Beautiful Summer Scenes Coloring Book
By Mindful Coloring Books

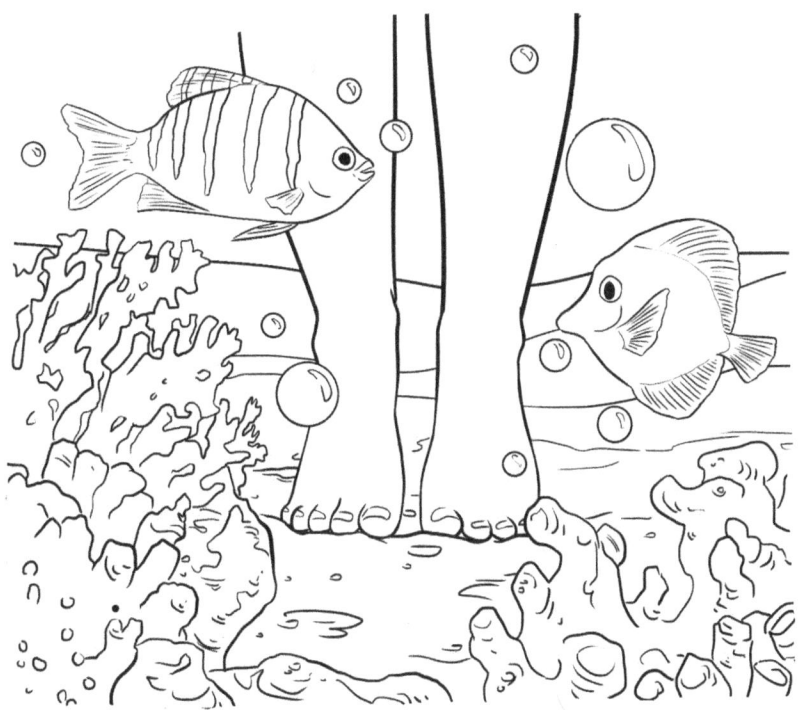

Coloring Tips

~ Sometimes what you think the color will look like and what it will actually look like are very different. Use the color test page.

~ Don't press too hard. Start out coloring lightly and you can always go back and make it darker.

~ Keep your pencil tips sharp so you can get into all the intricate spaces.

~ Using markers? Place a scrap piece of paper behind the page you are coloring. Pages in this book are only printed on one side but there is still the risk of bleed through to the next page.

~ Try different coloring utensils marketed for adults. It is fun and quality can vary greatly.

COLOR TEST PAGE

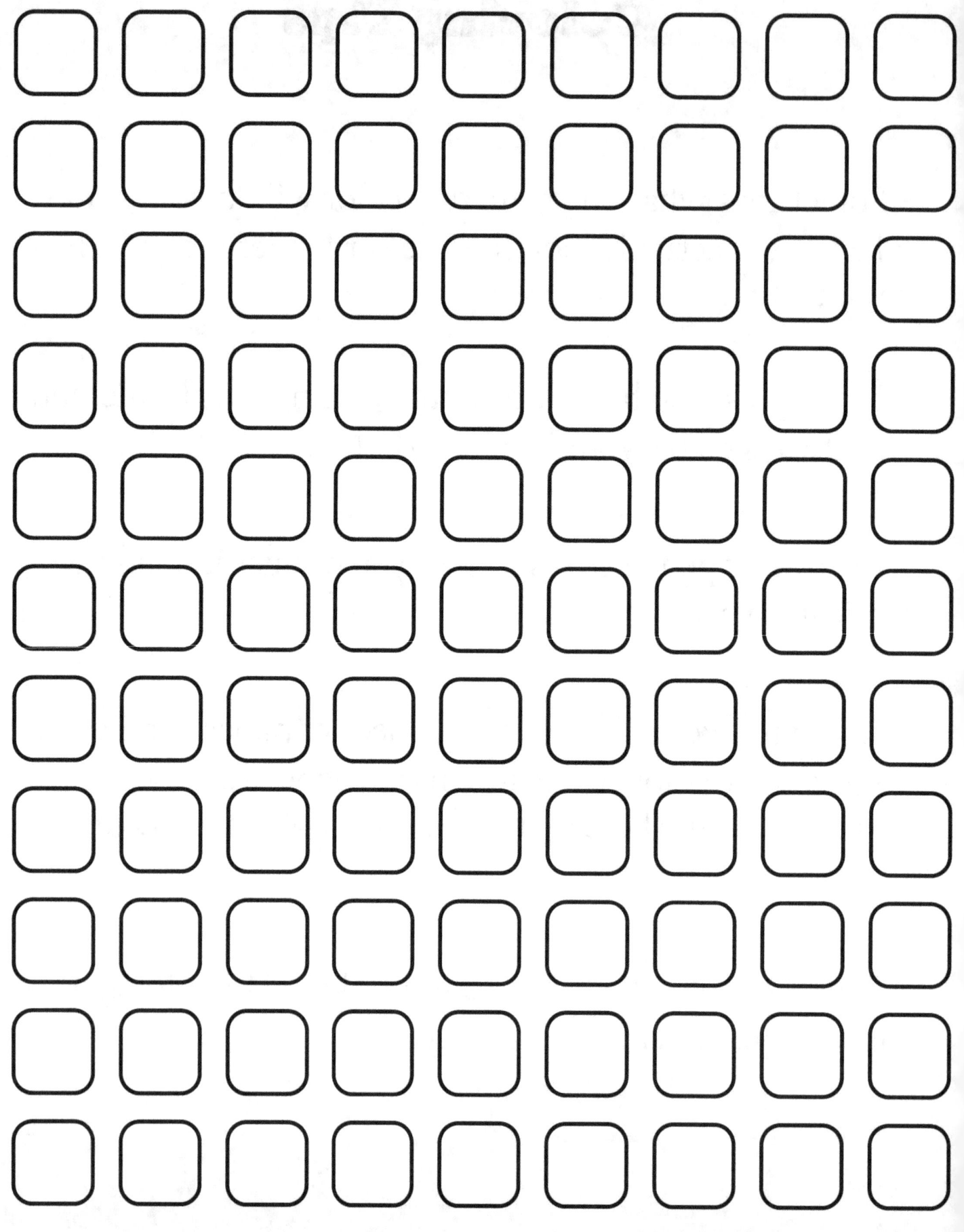

COLOR TEST PAGE

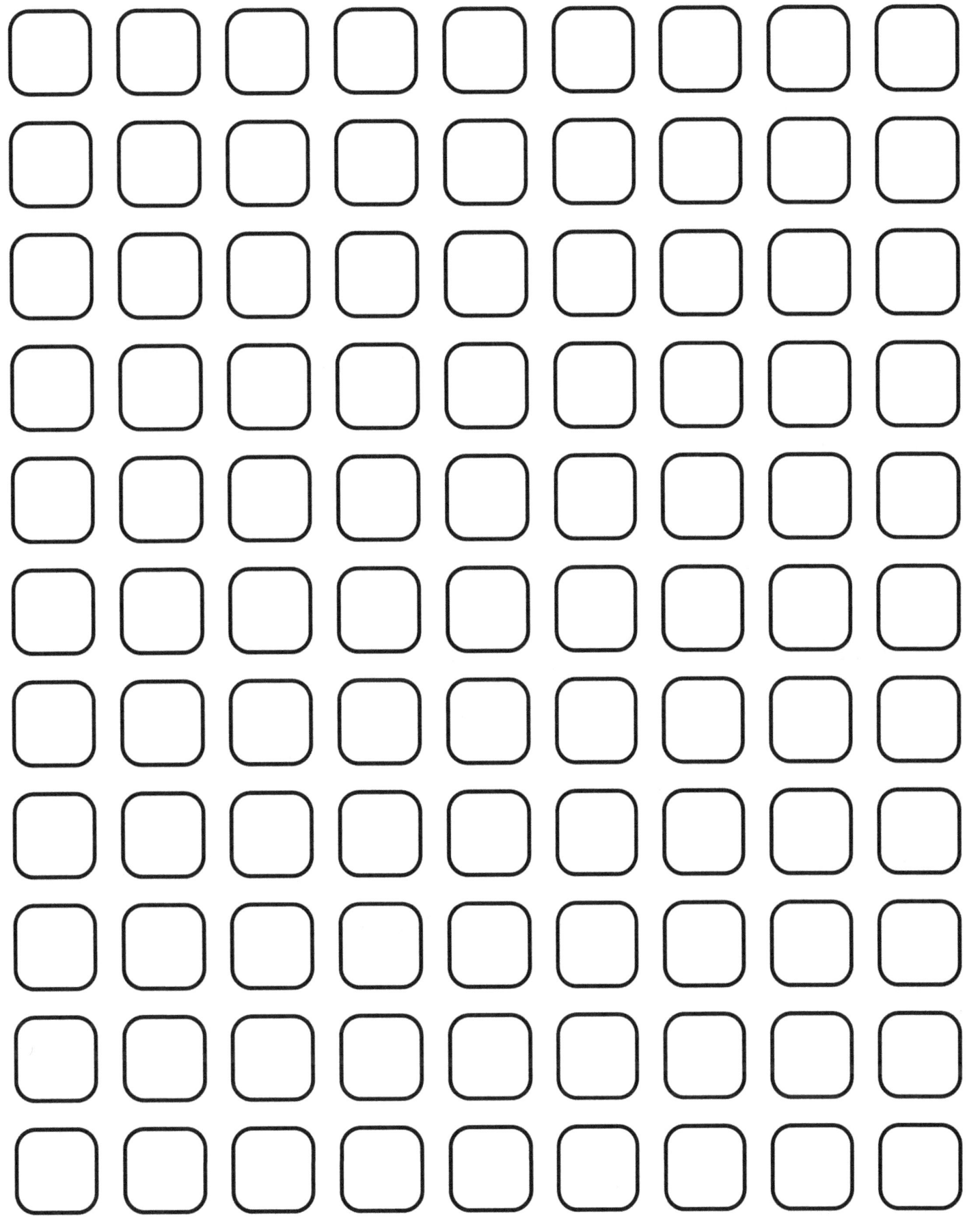

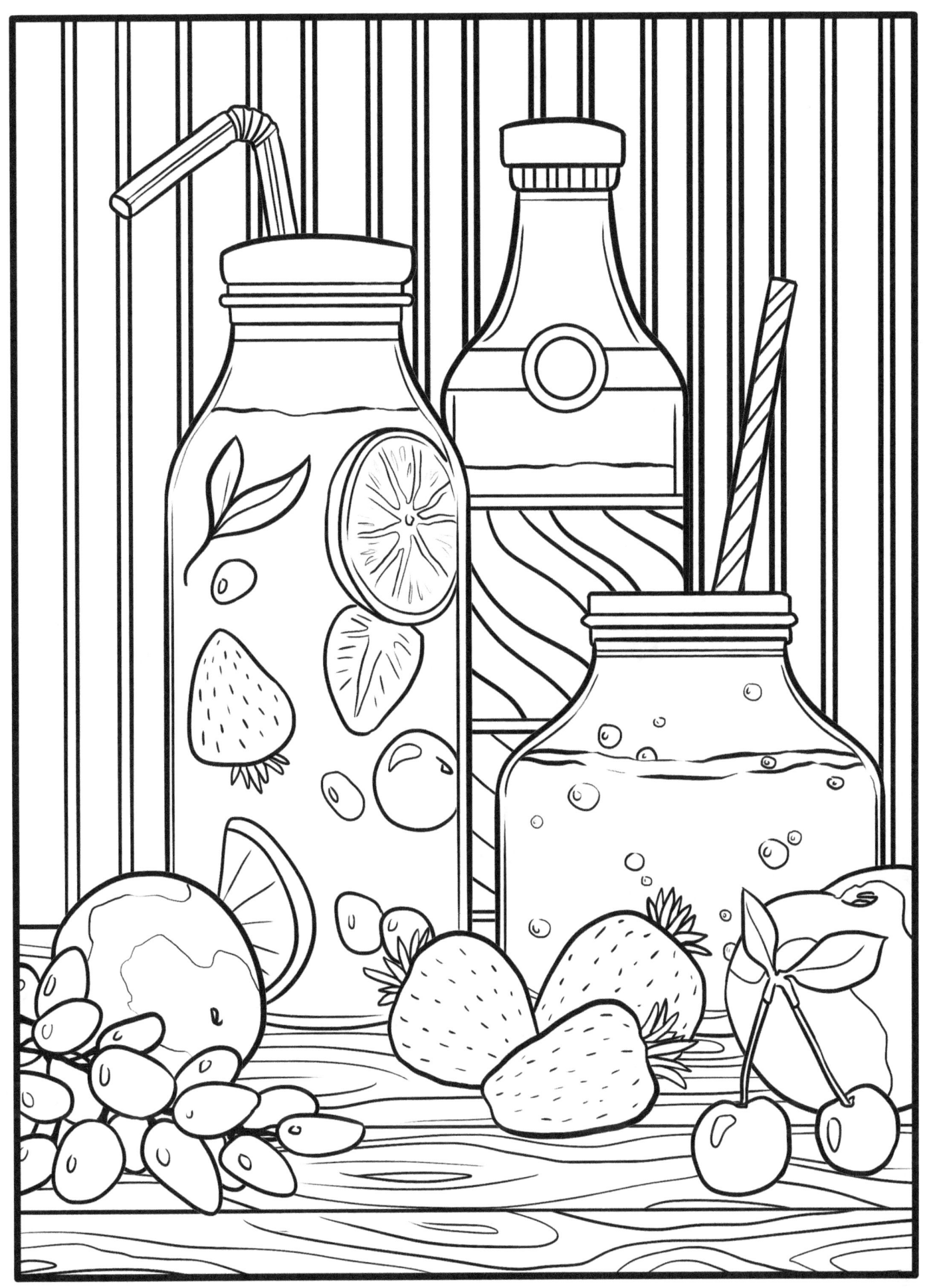

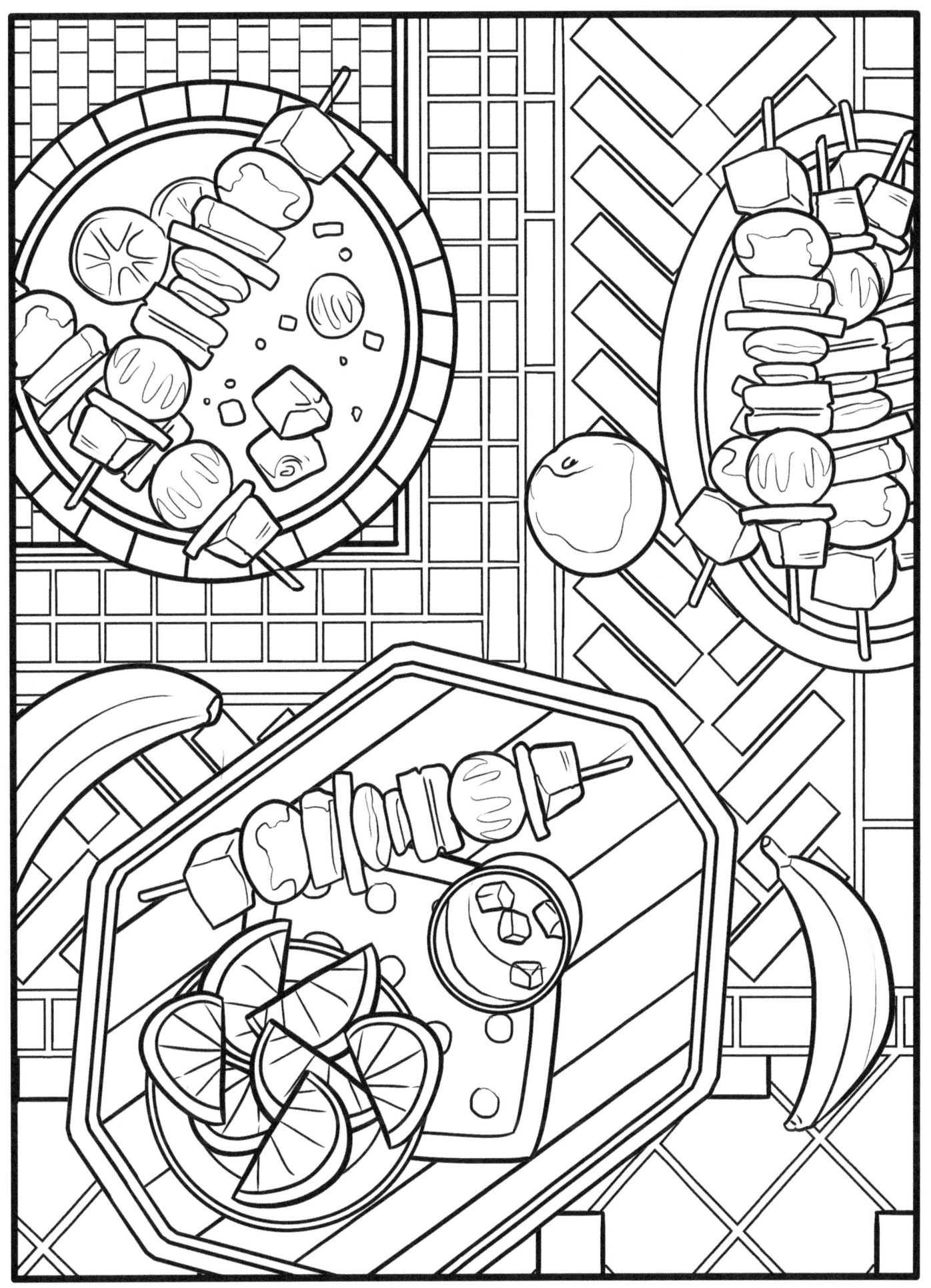

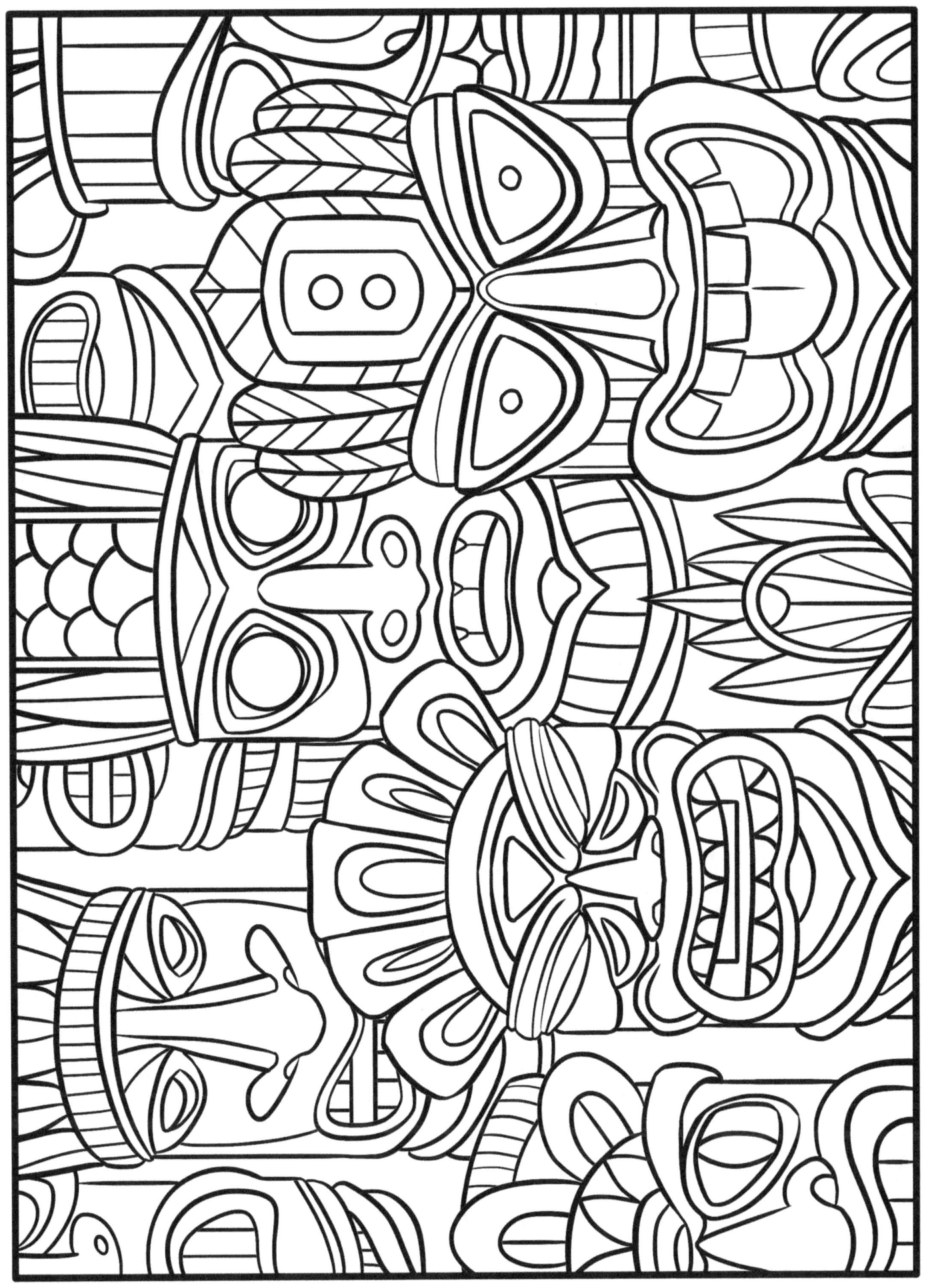

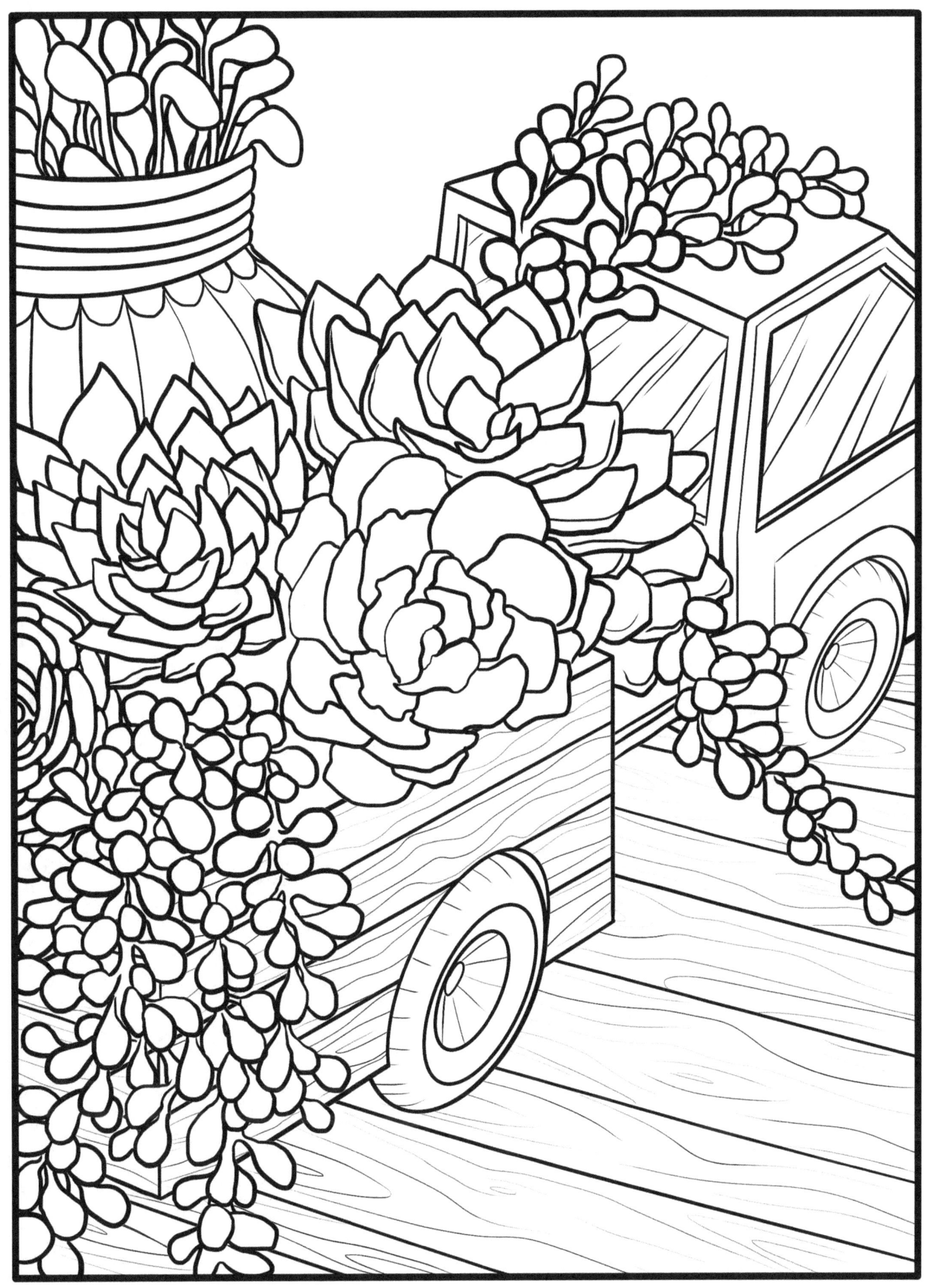

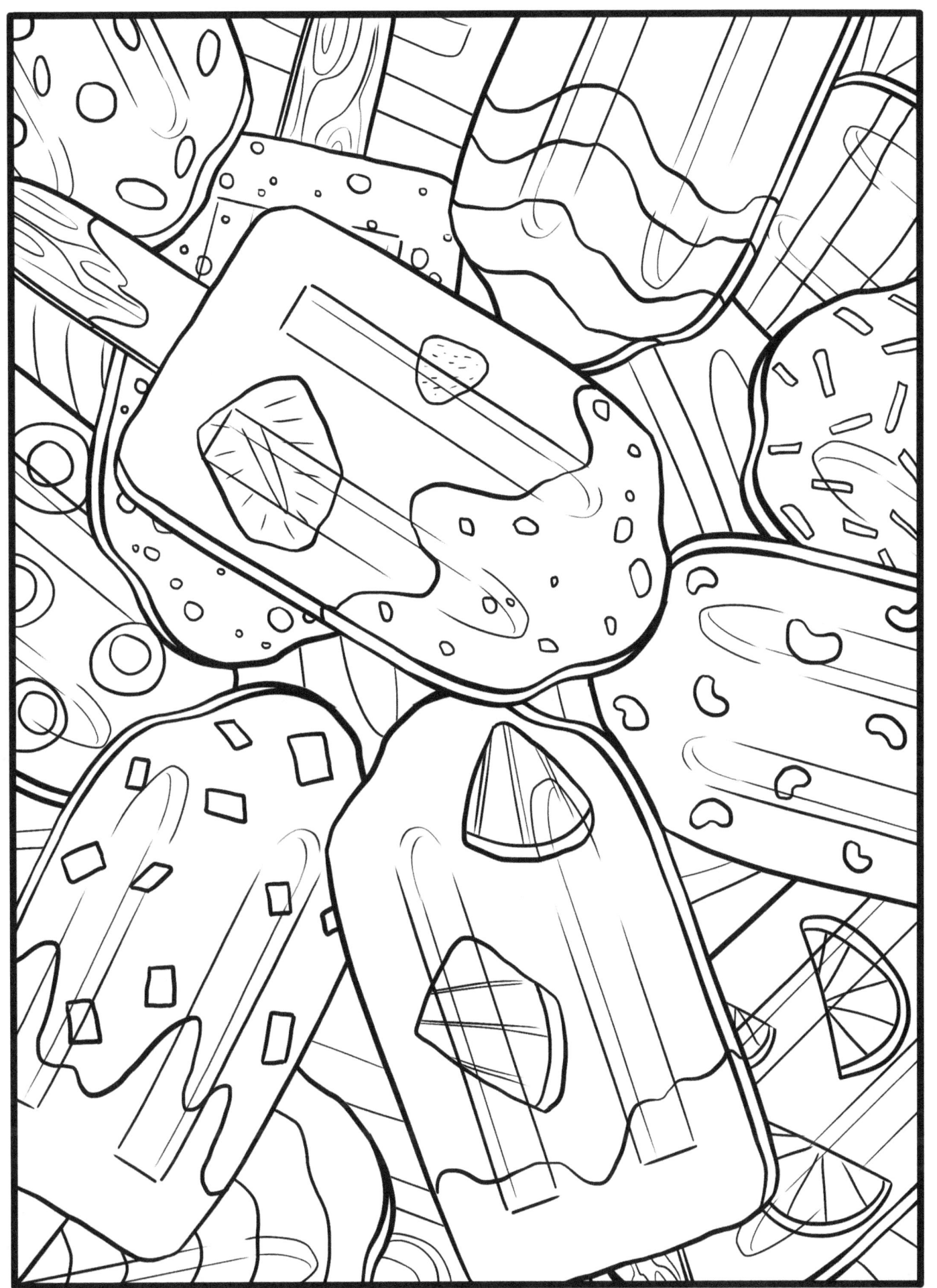

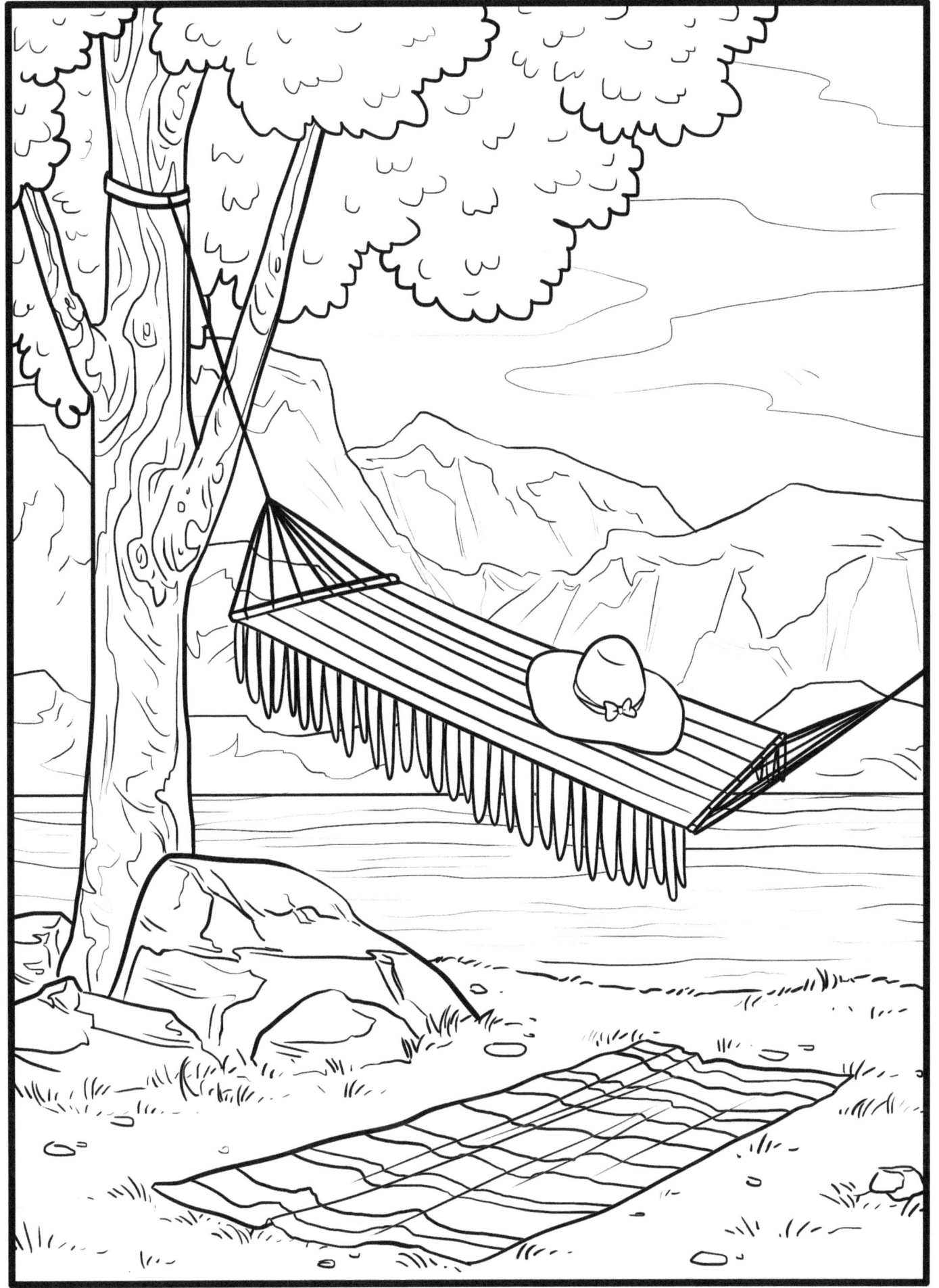

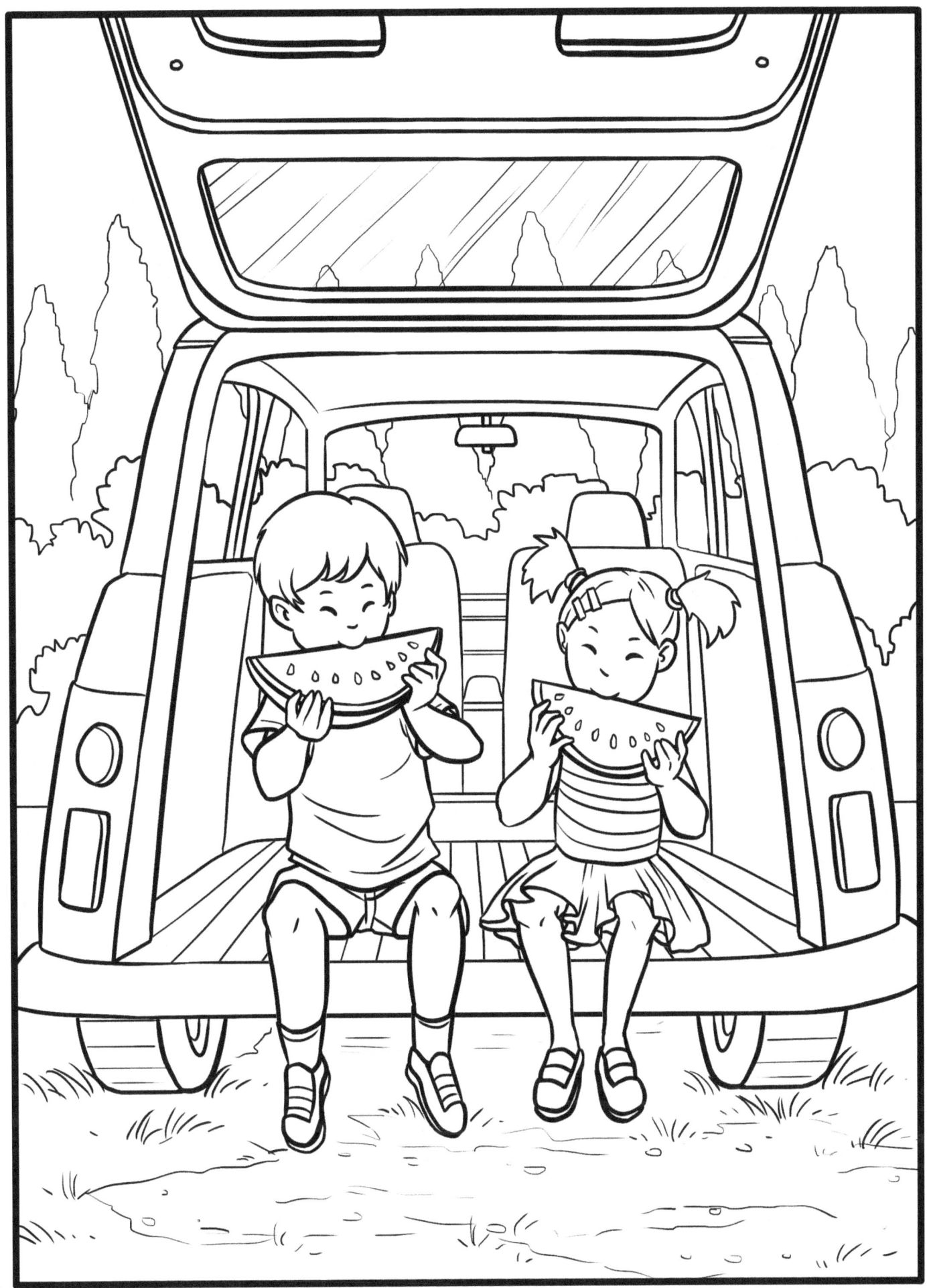

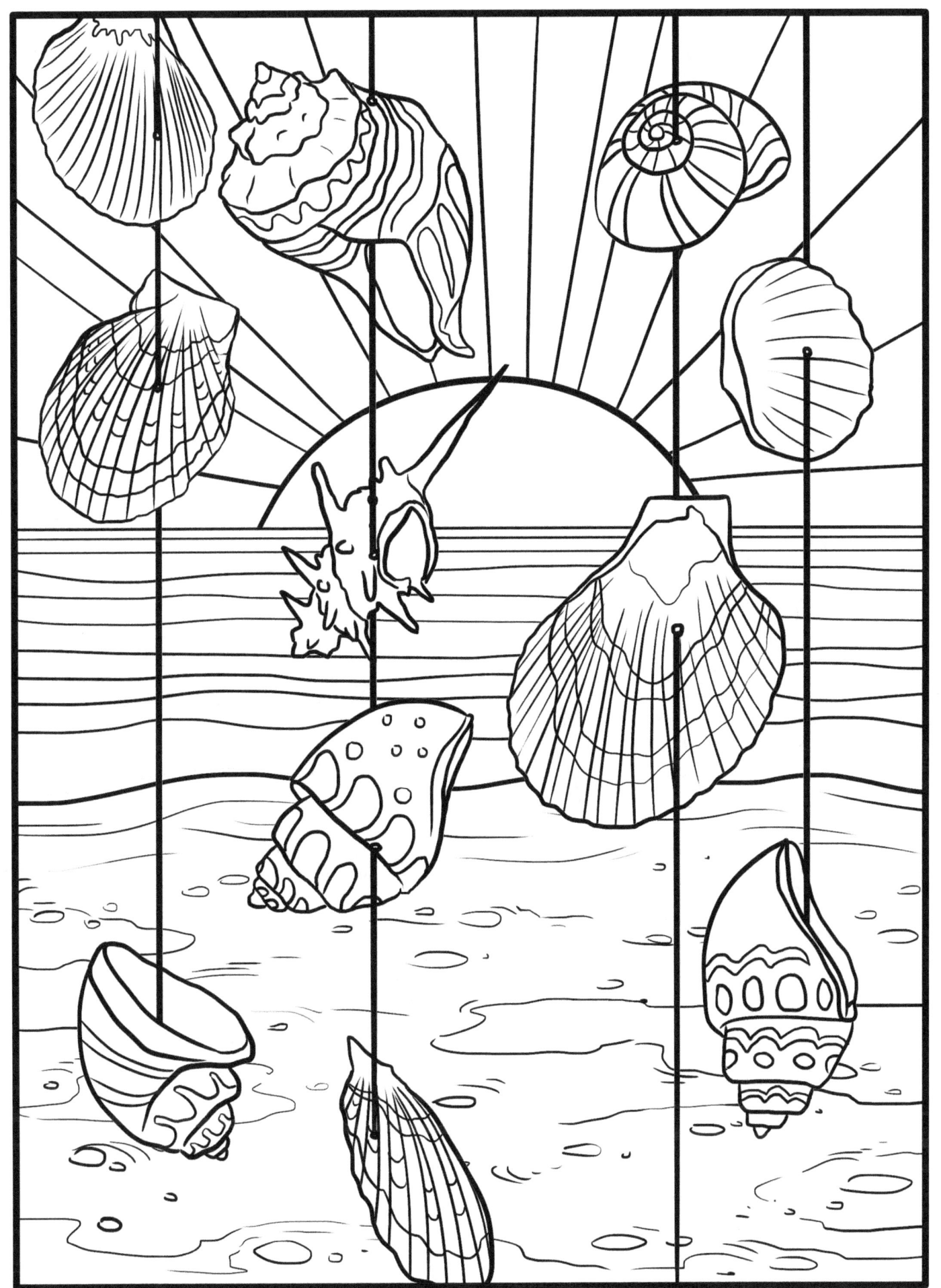

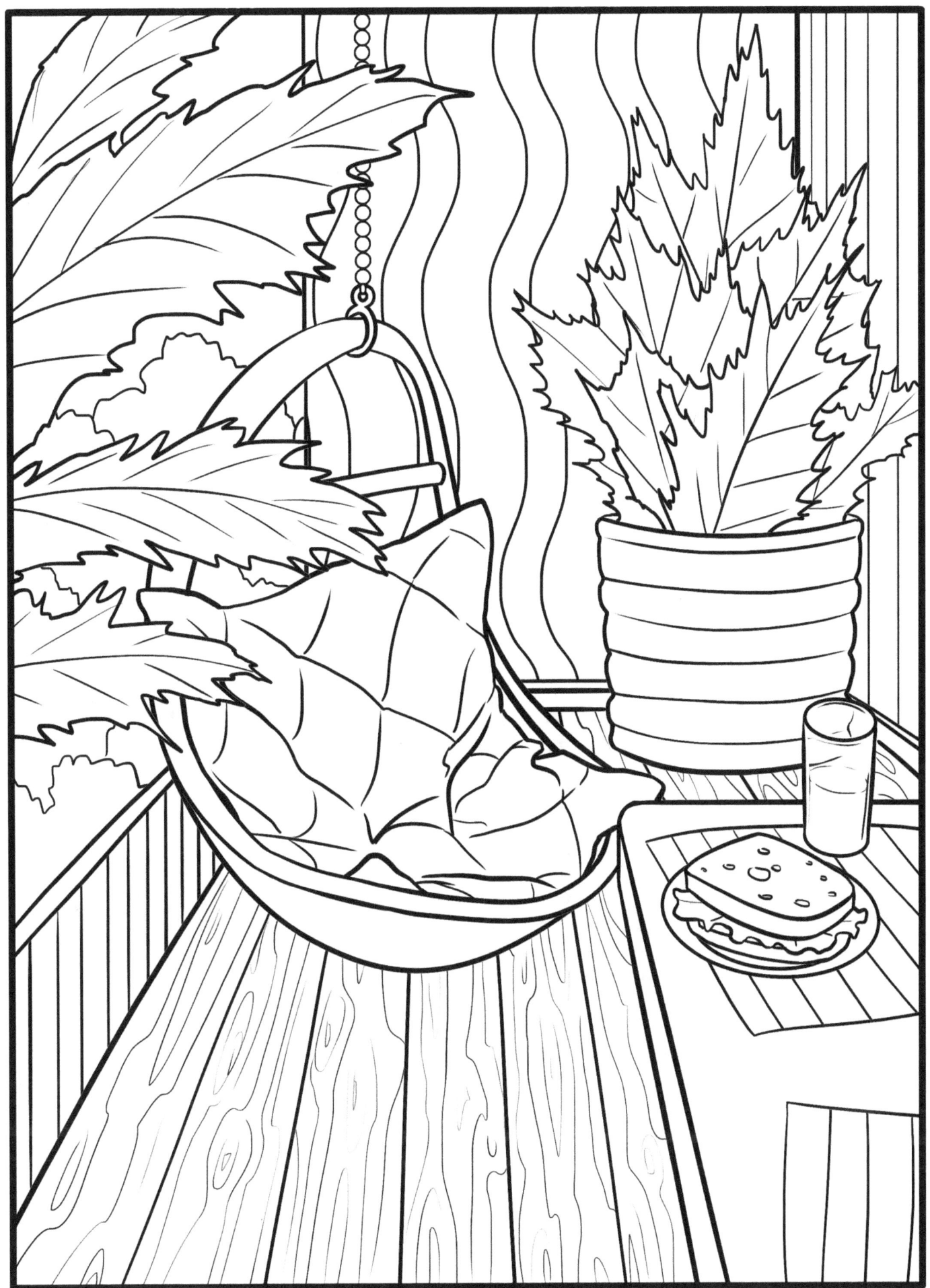

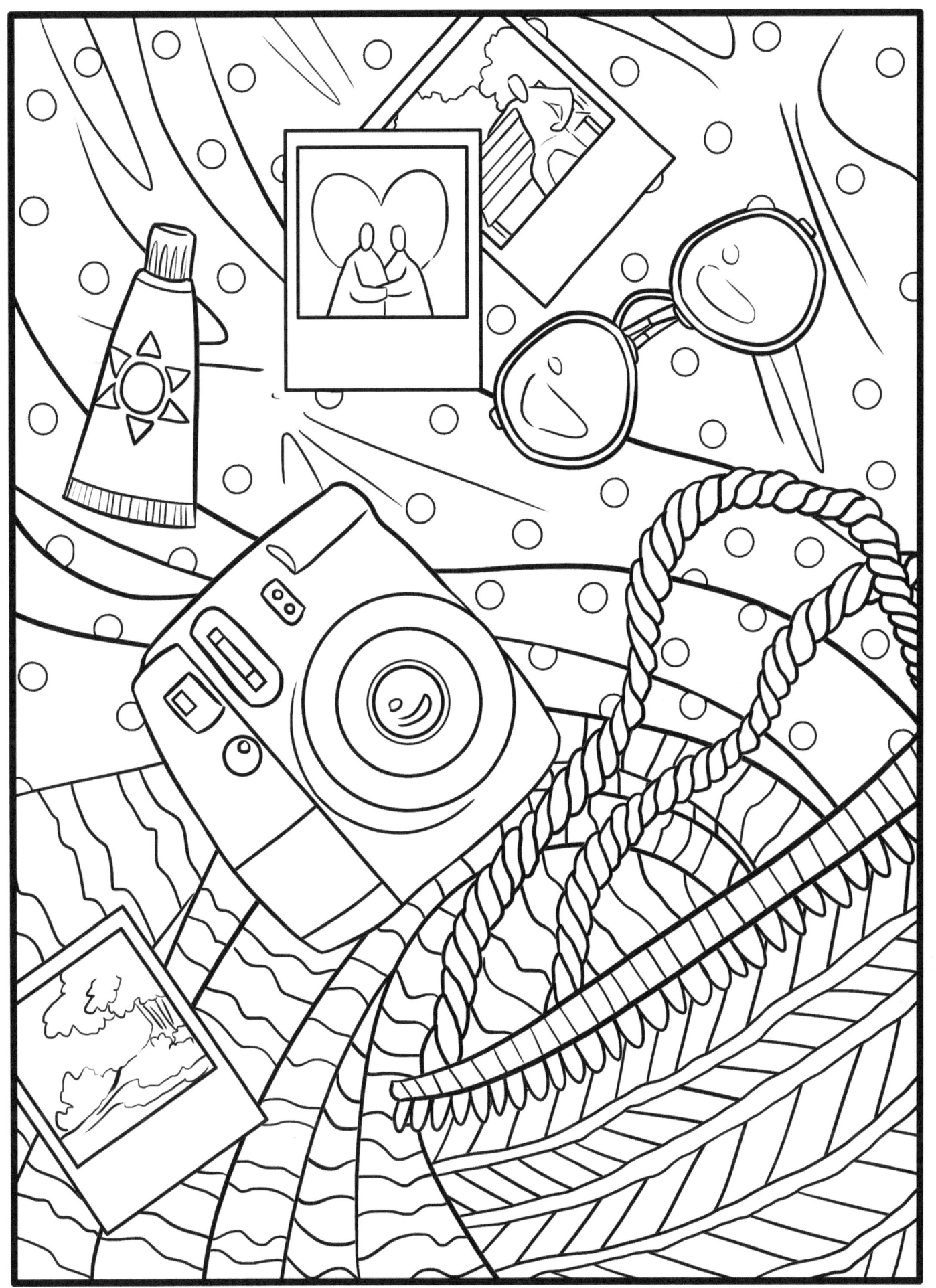

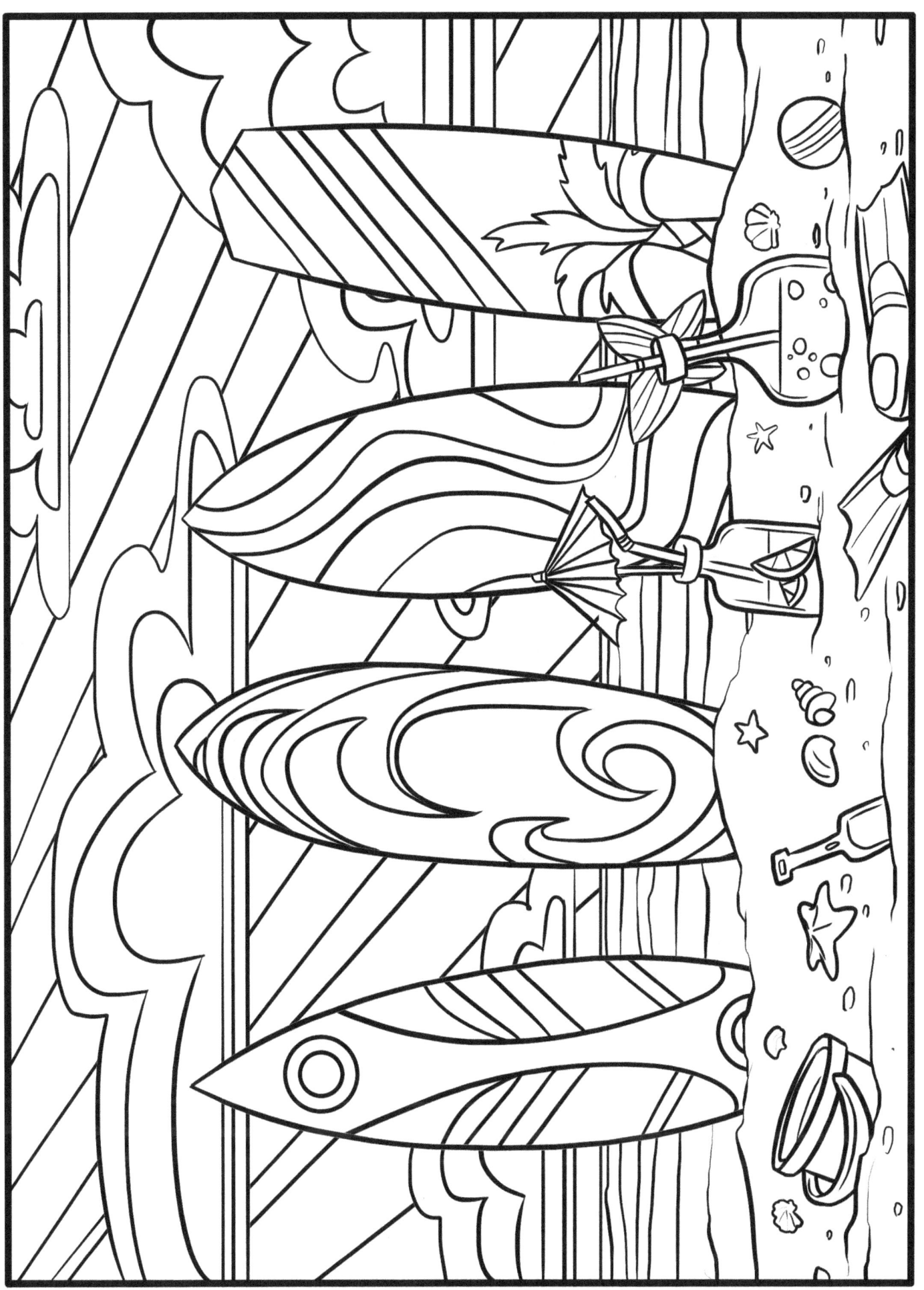

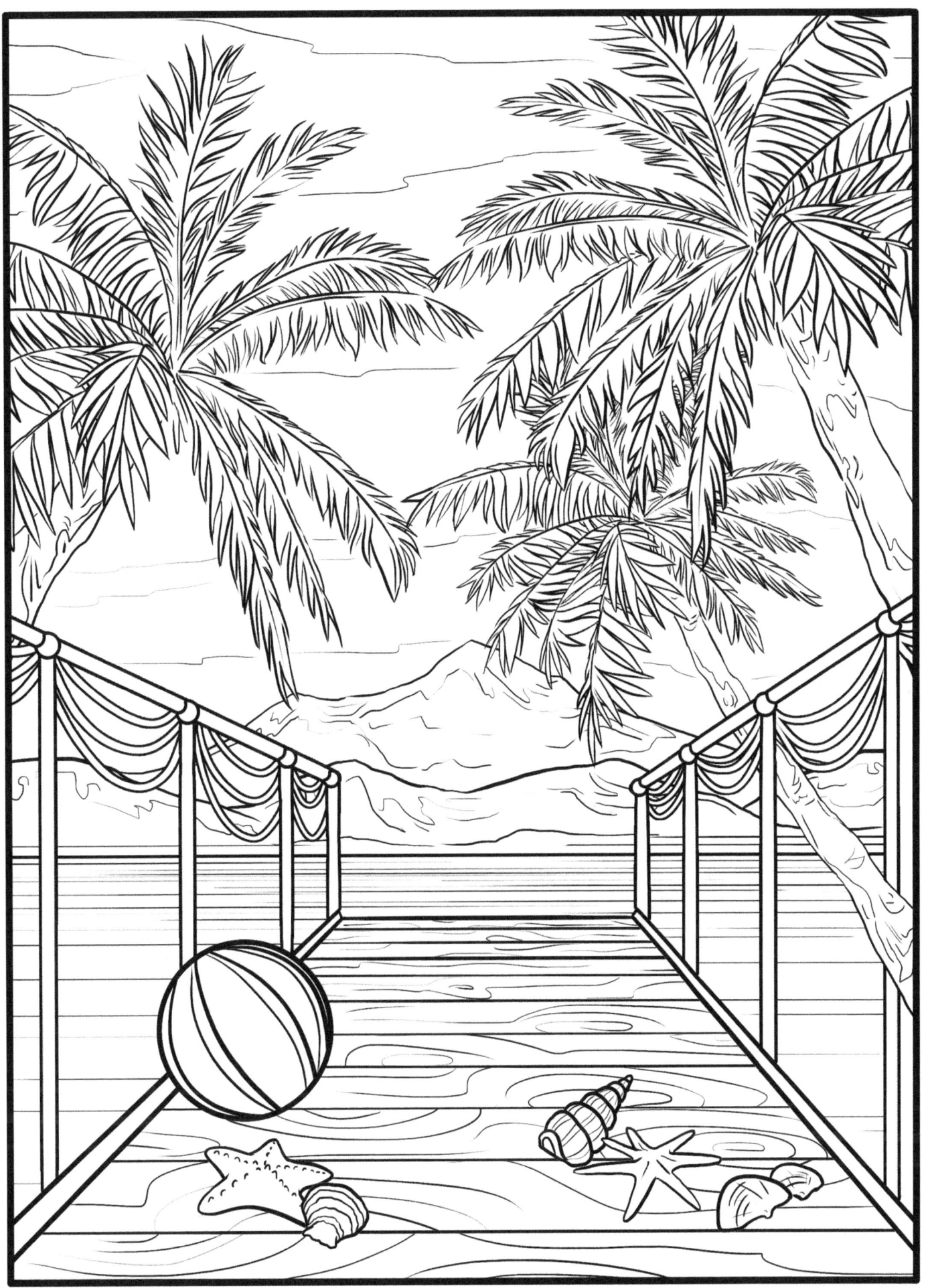

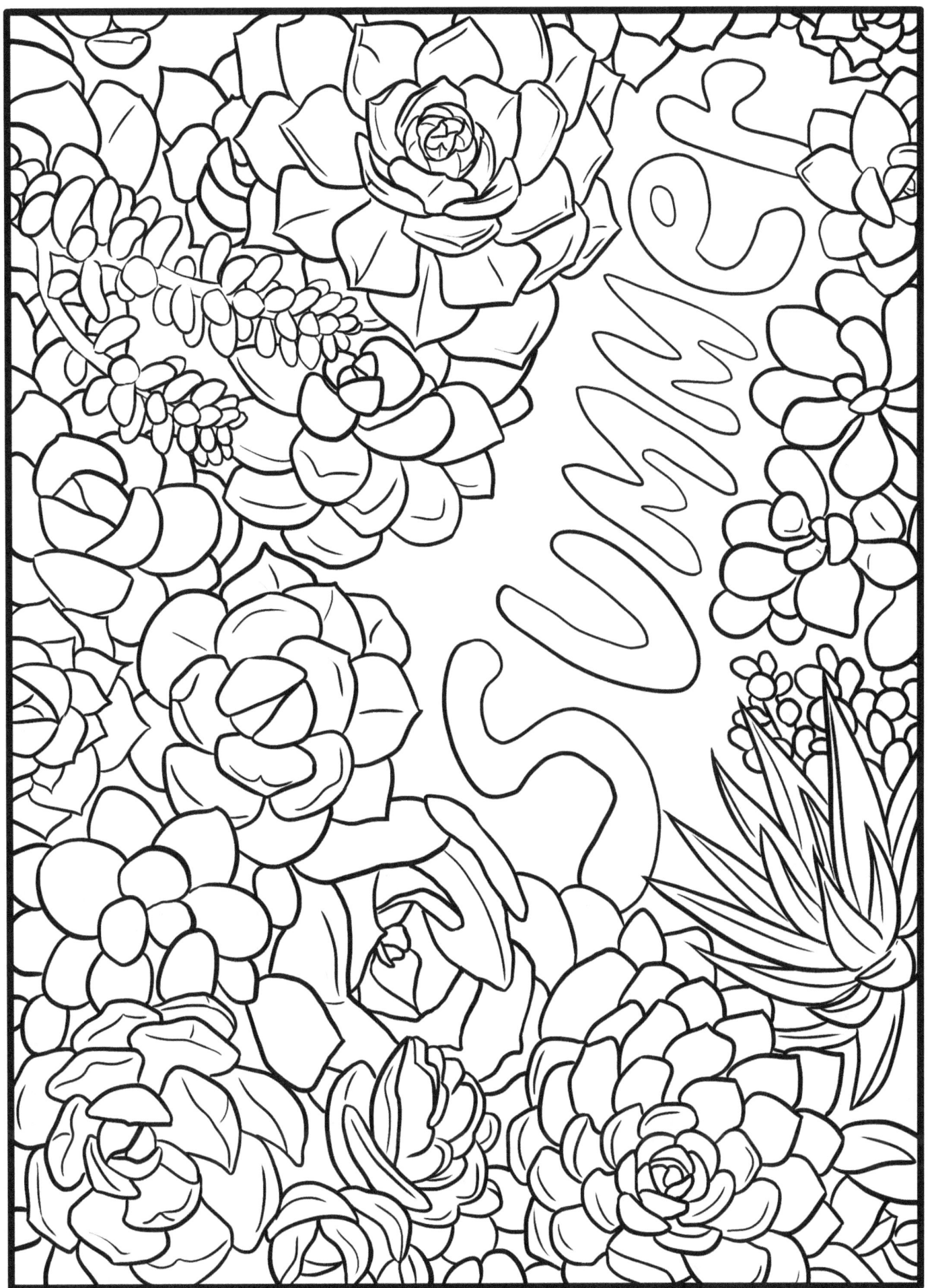

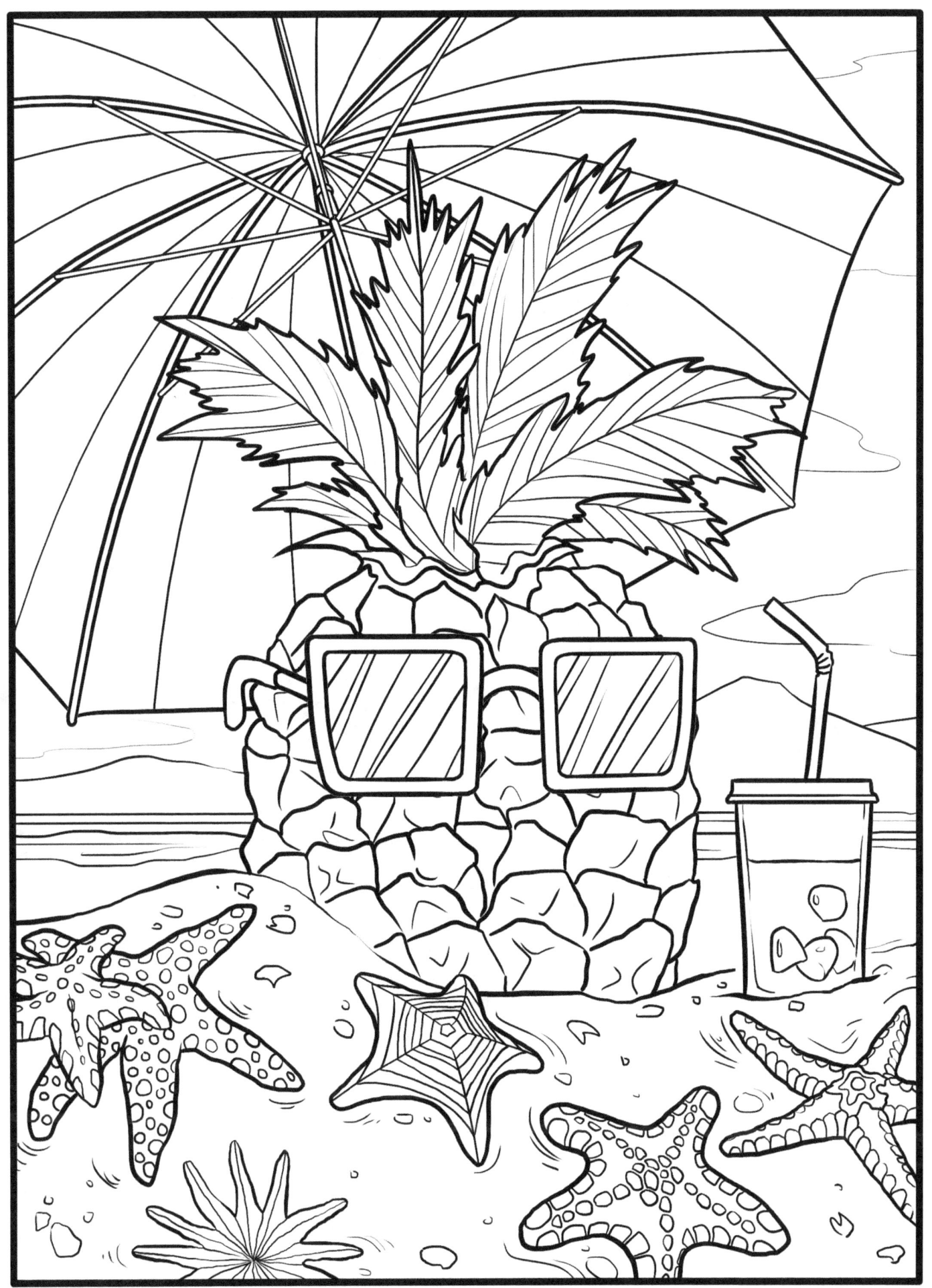

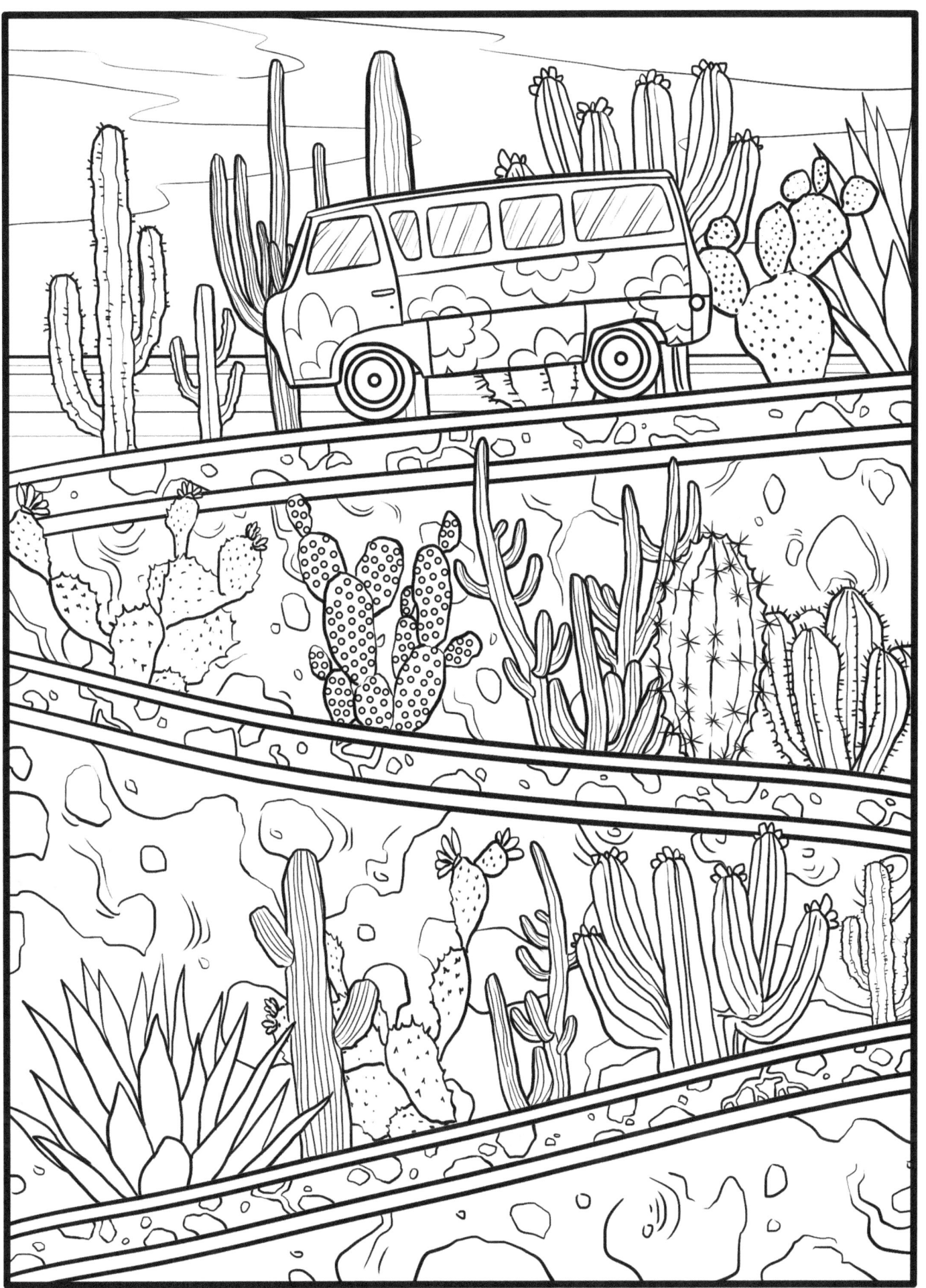

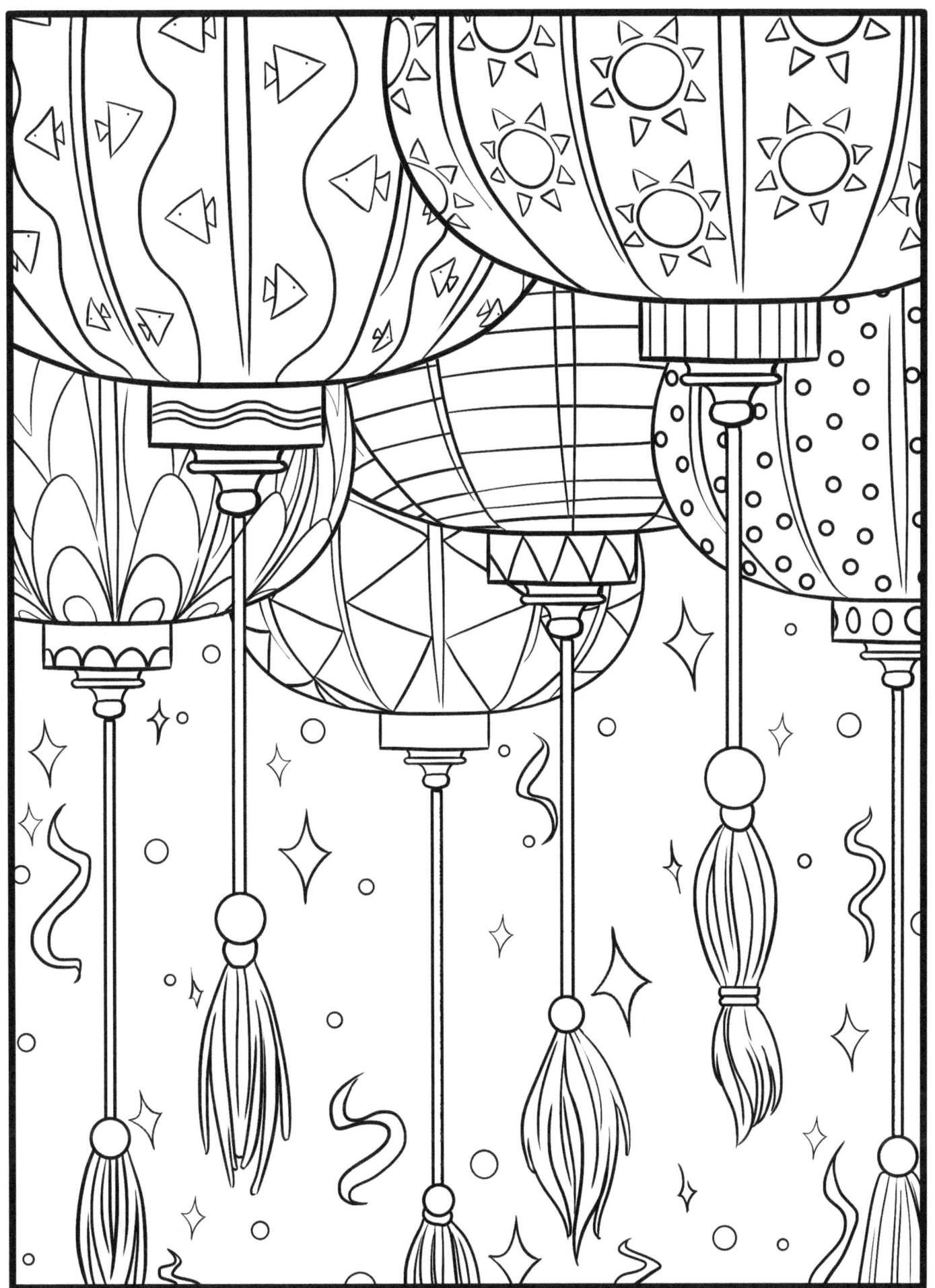

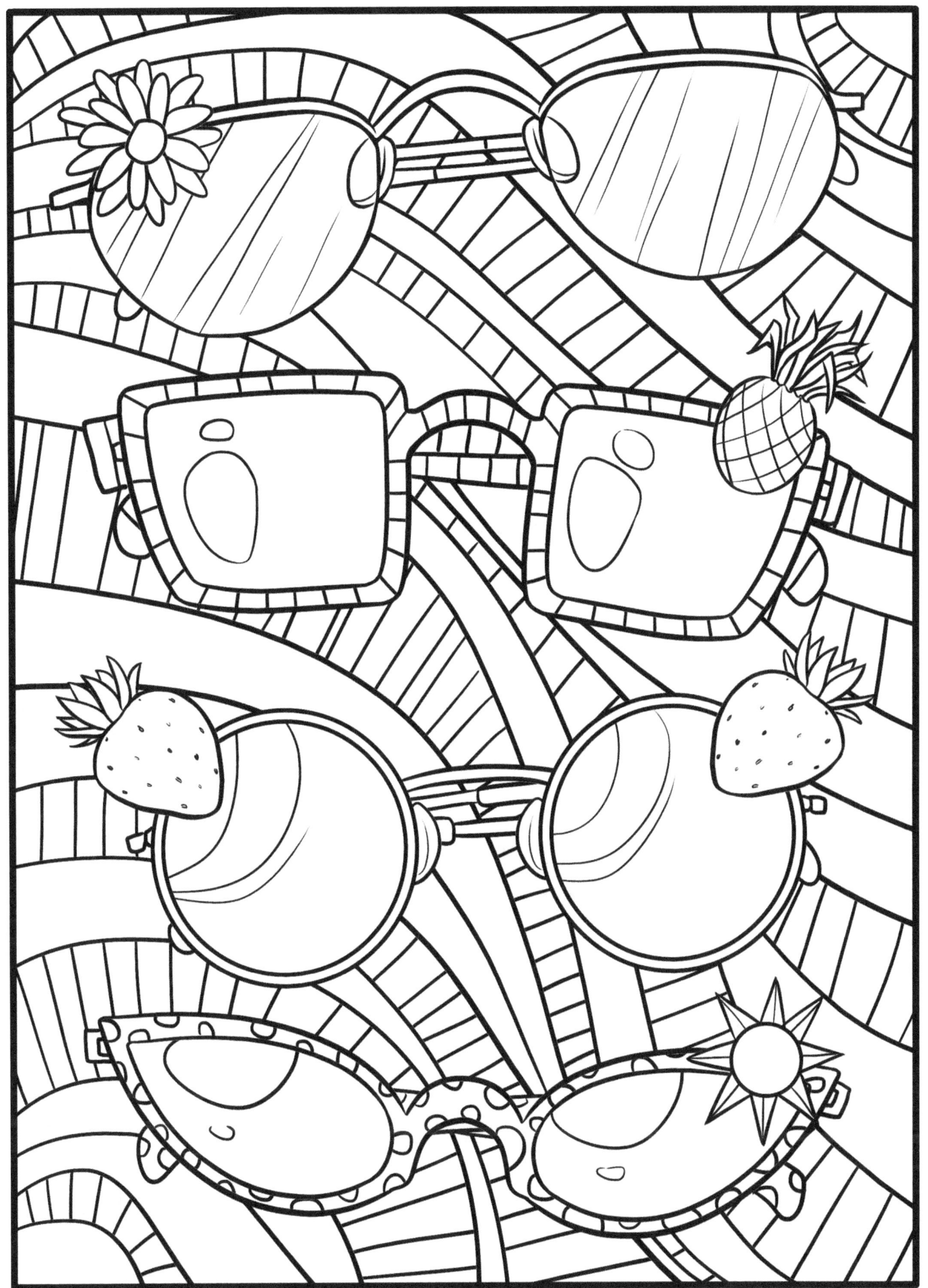

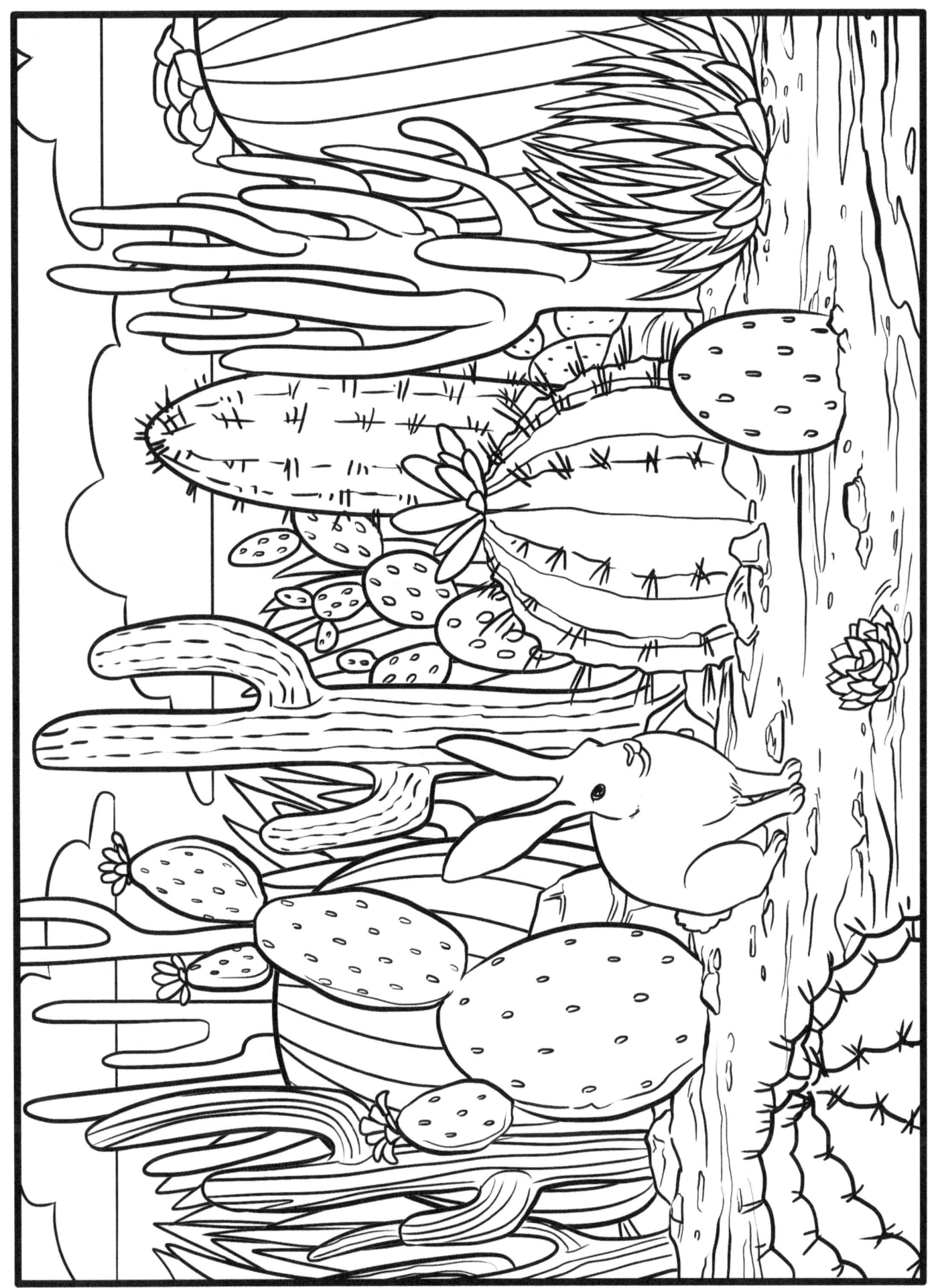

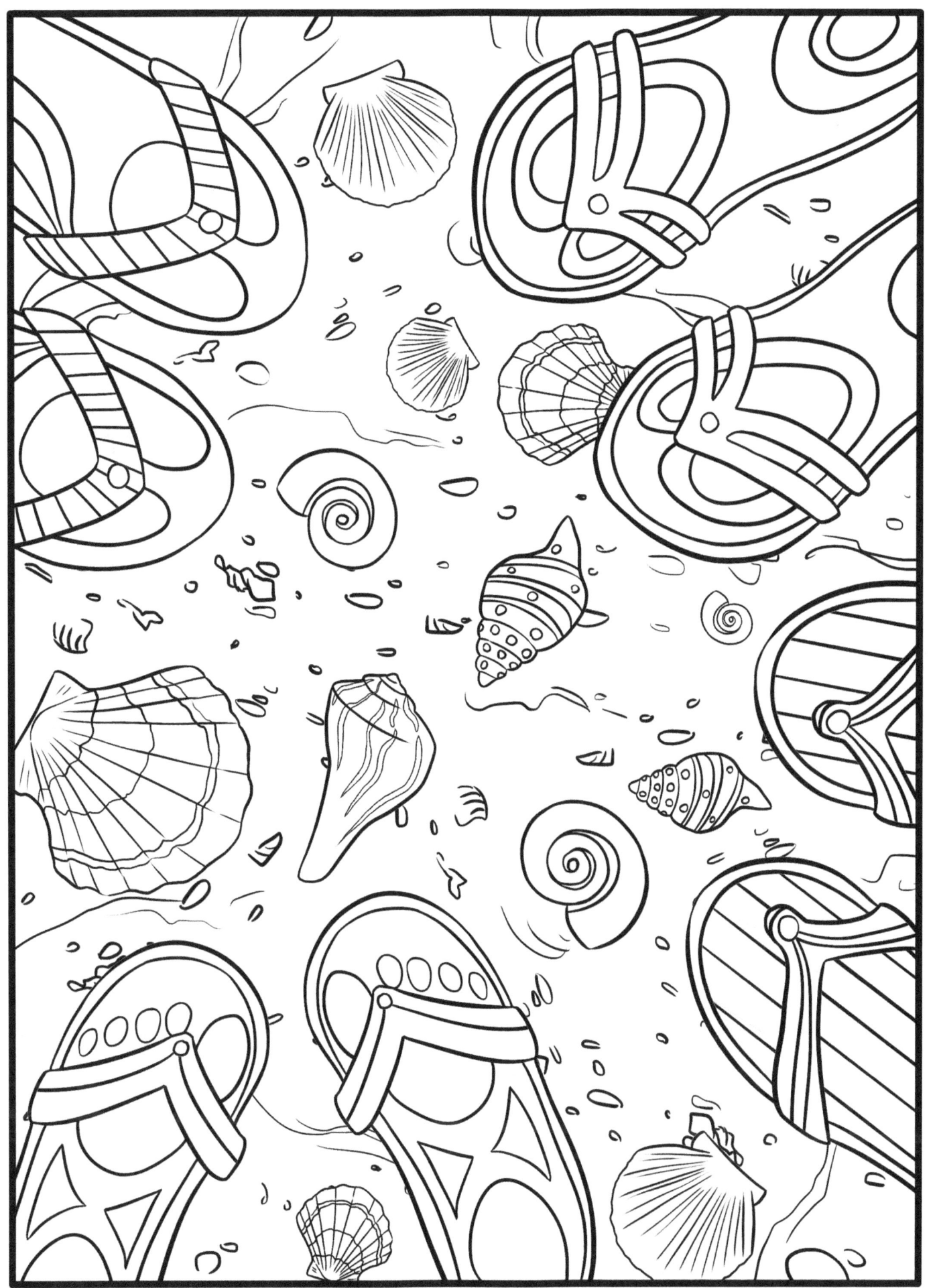

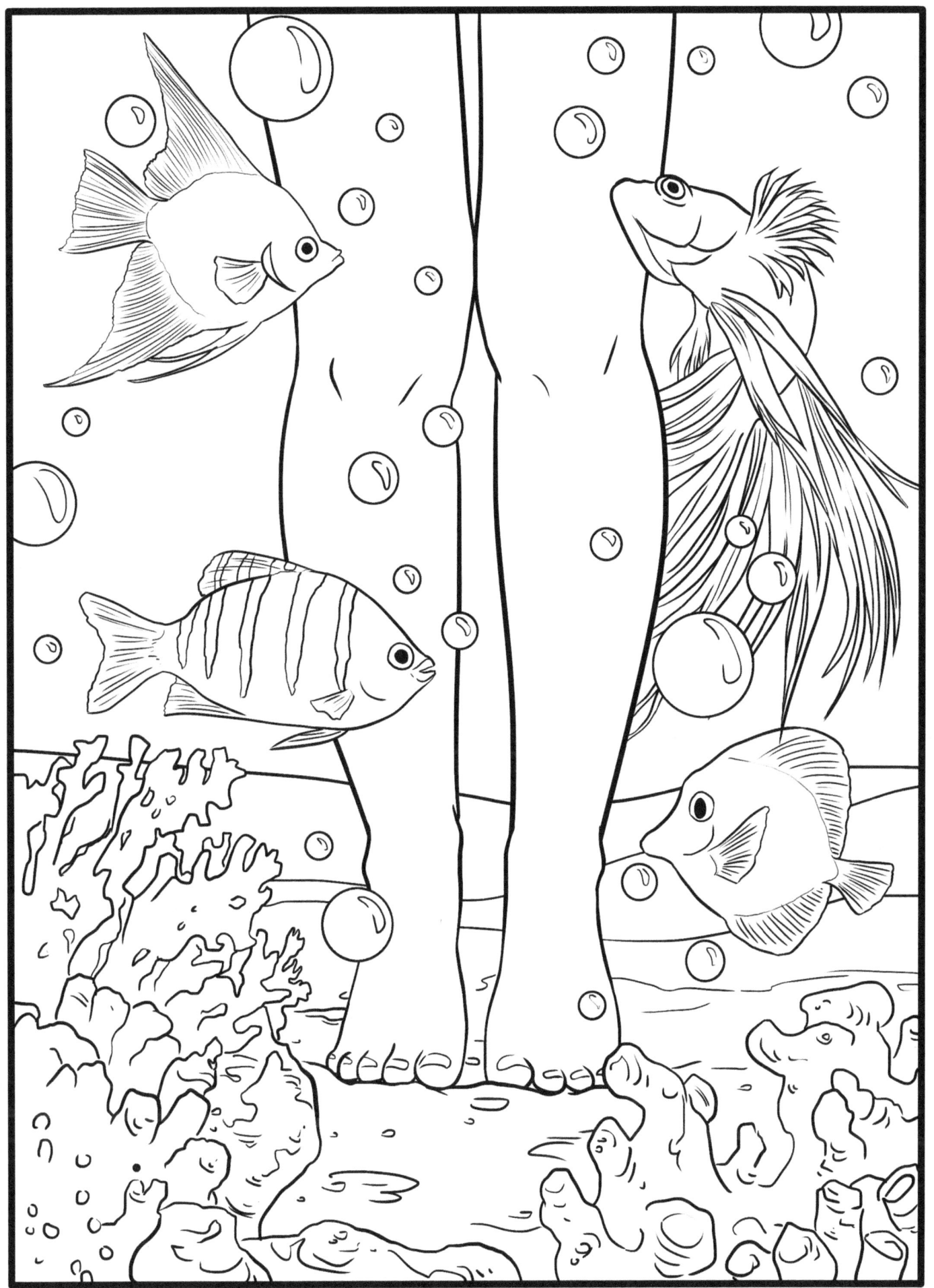

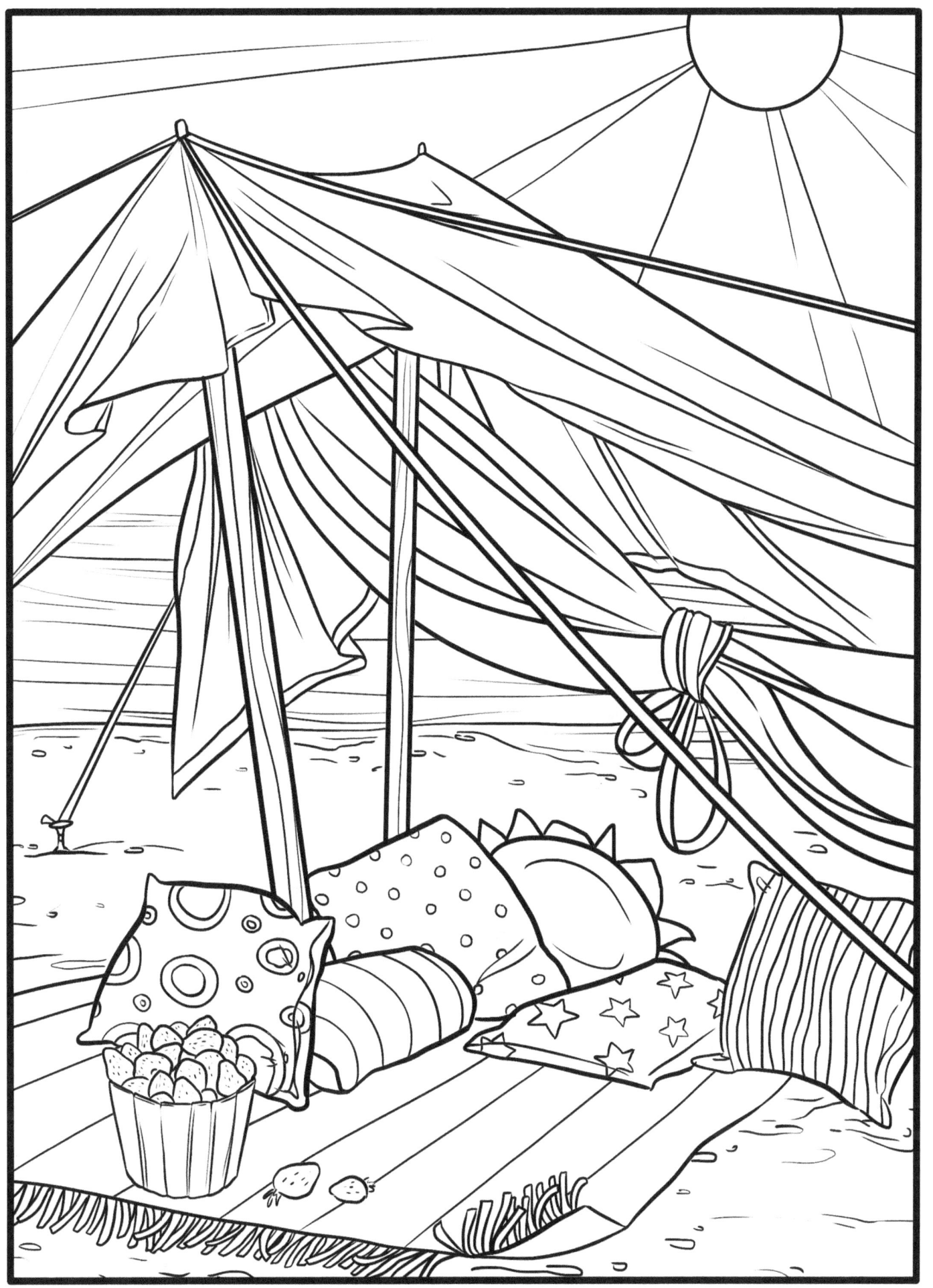

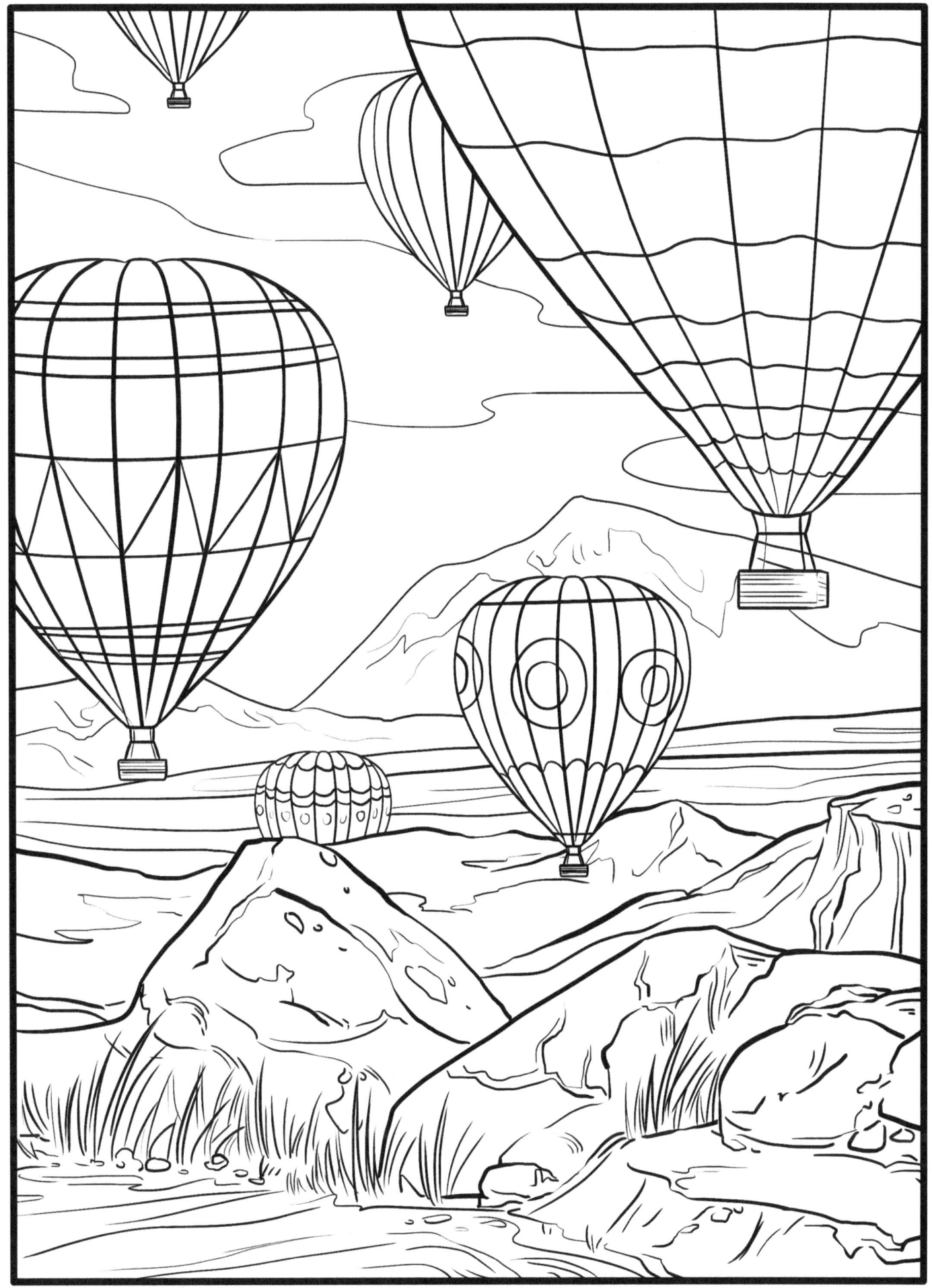

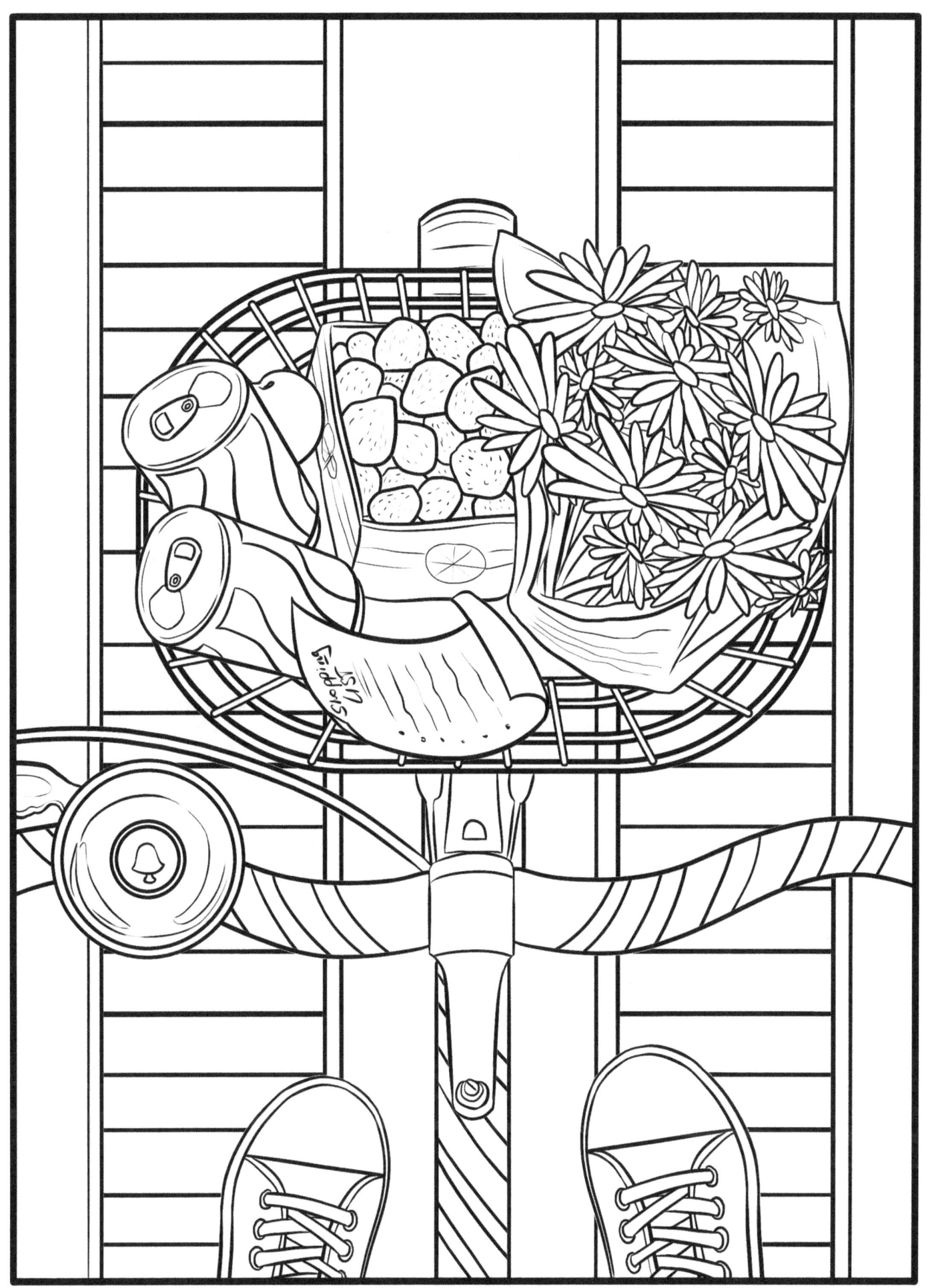

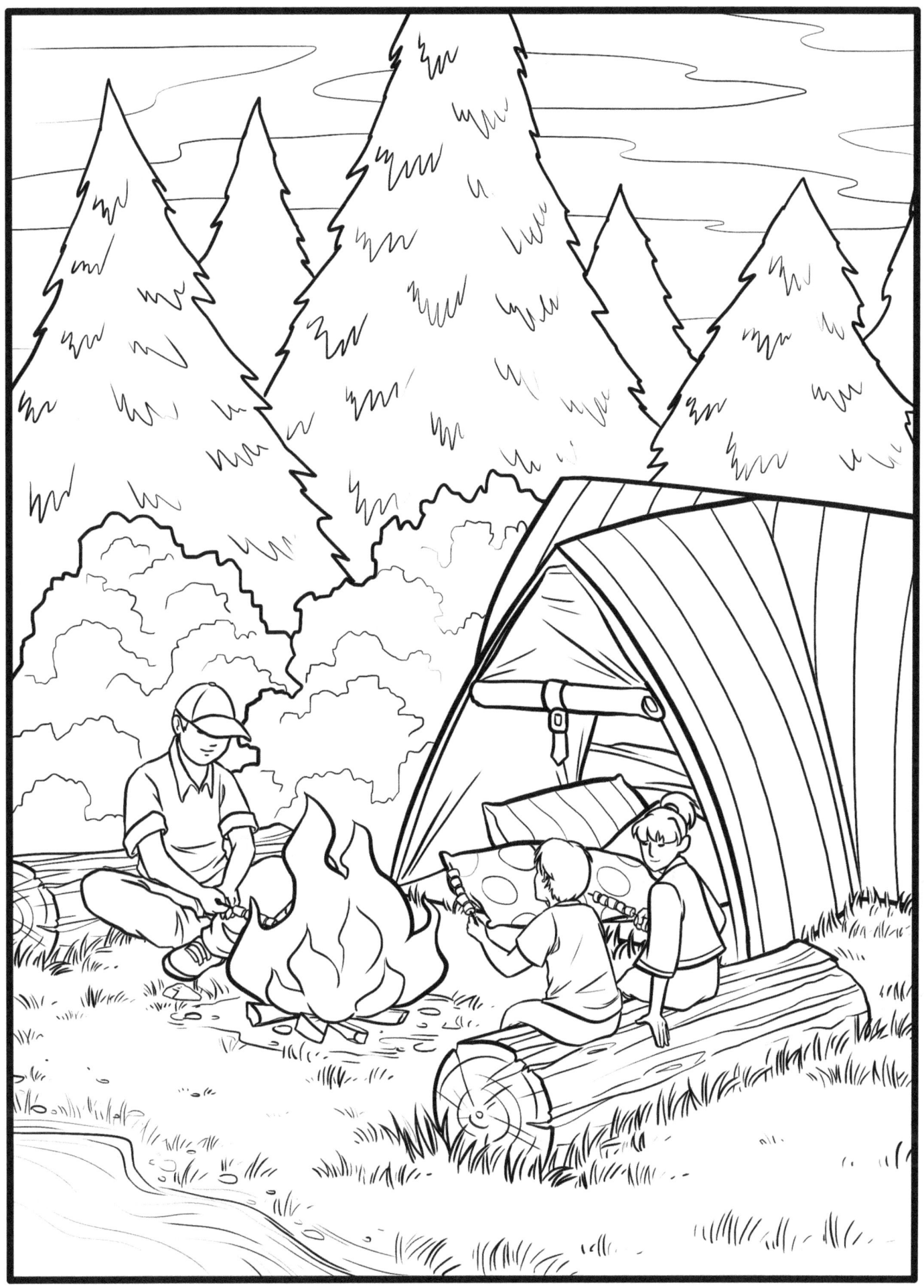

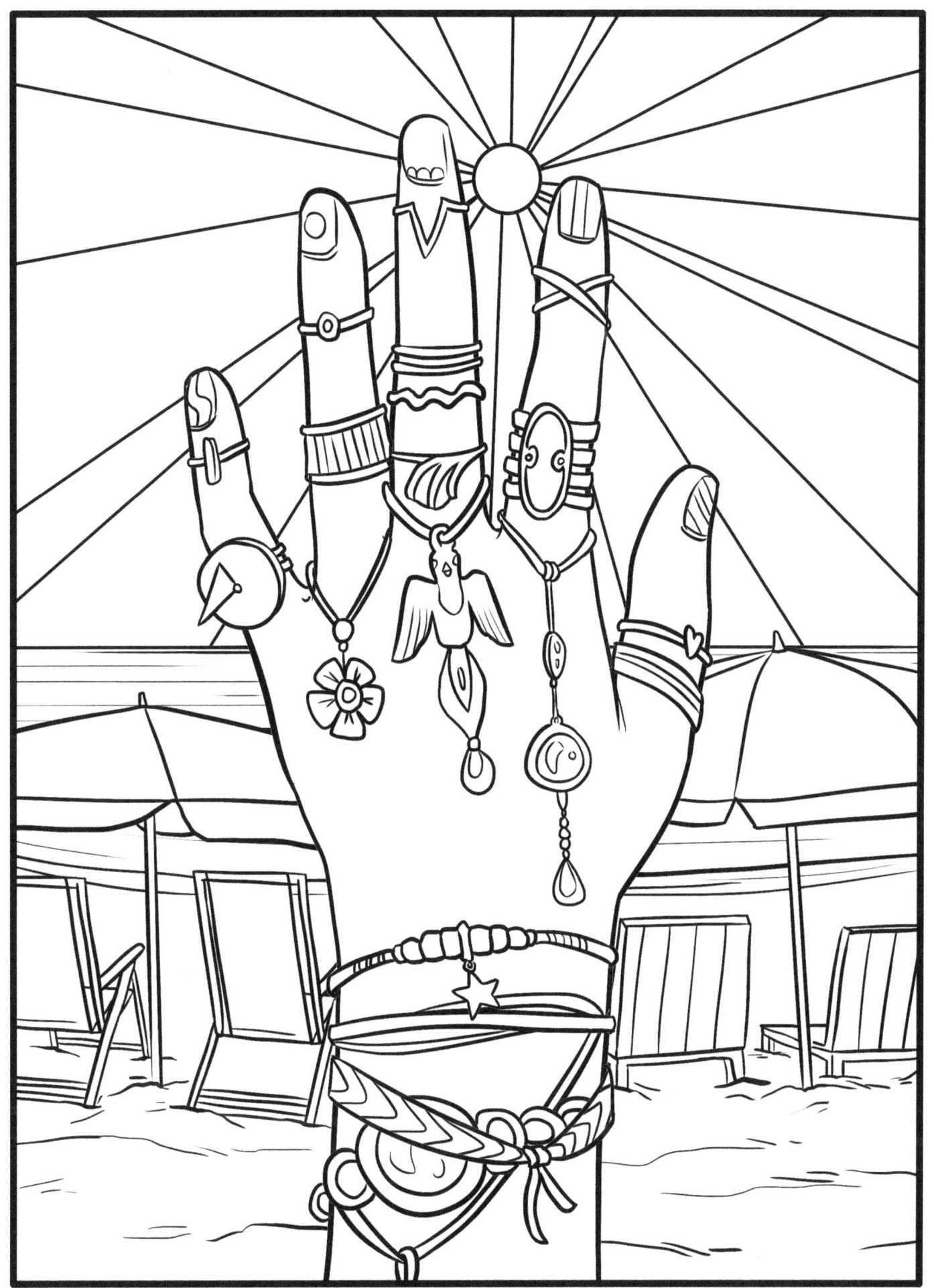

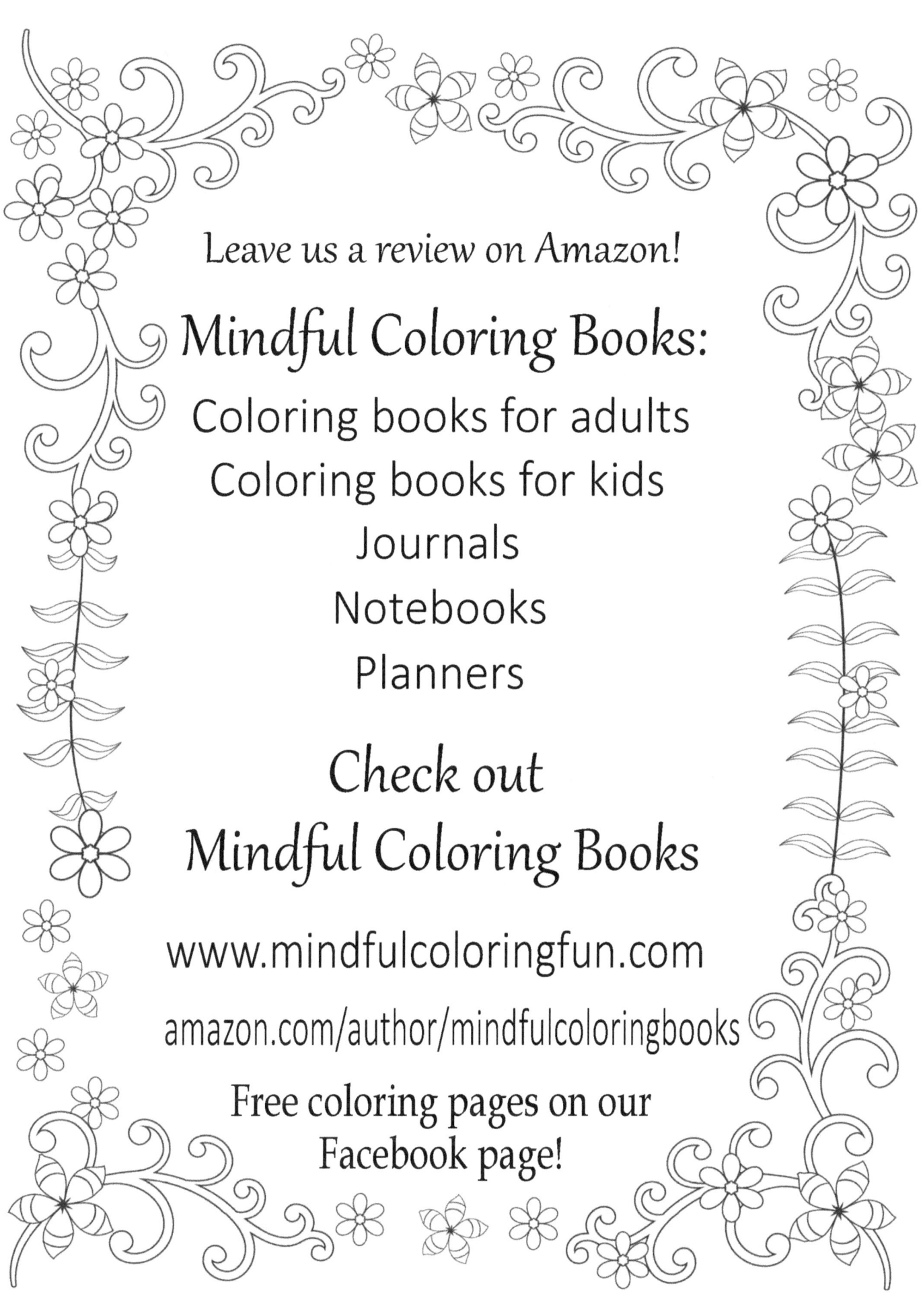

Leave us a review on Amazon!

Mindful Coloring Books:

Coloring books for adults

Coloring books for kids

Journals

Notebooks

Planners

Check out
Mindful Coloring Books

www.mindfulcoloringfun.com

amazon.com/author/mindfulcoloringbooks

Free coloring pages on our
Facebook page!

Enjoy these preview pages from some of our other coloring books!

Beautiful Spring Scenes
Coloring Book

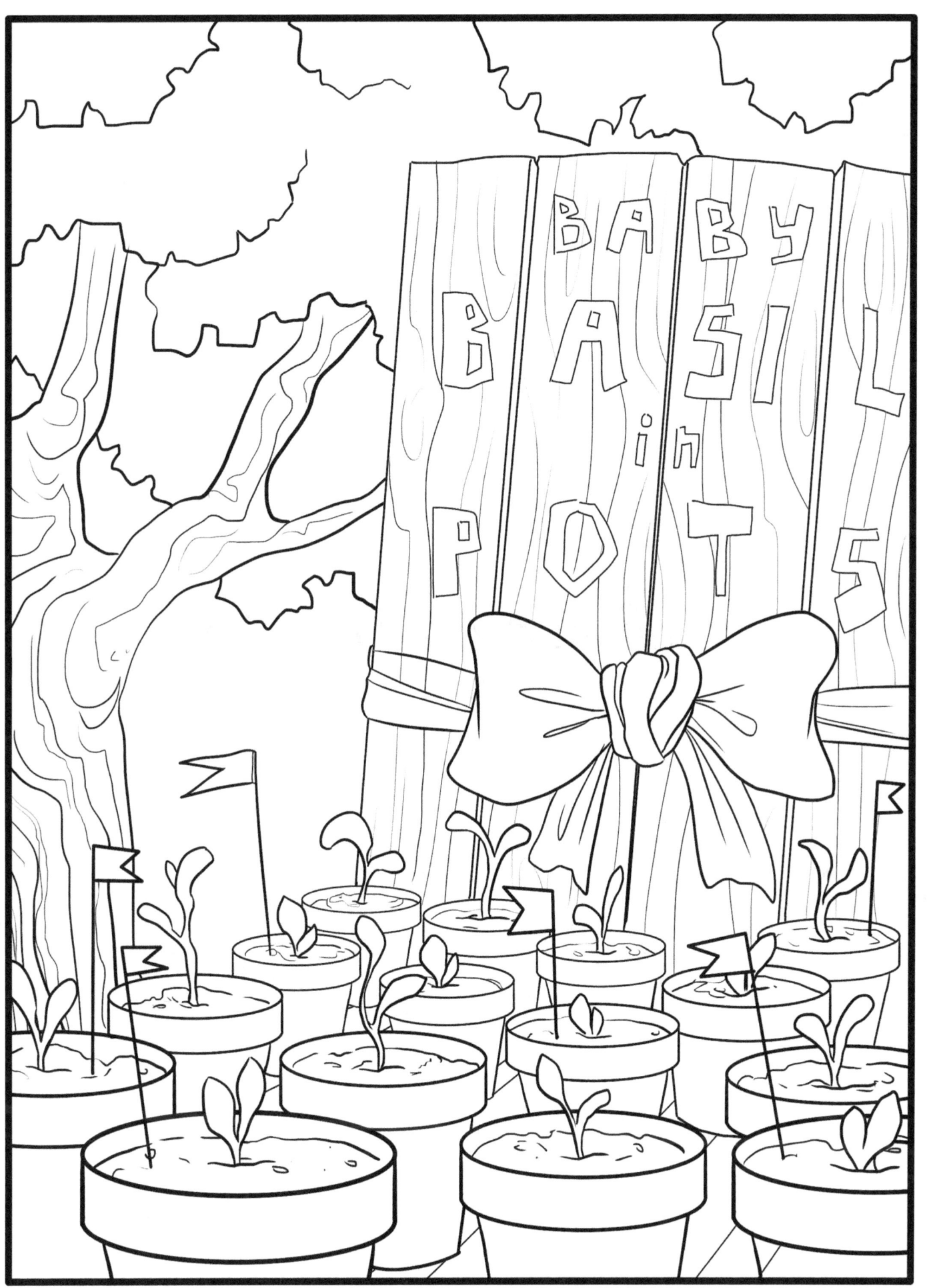

A Walk in the Winter Woods

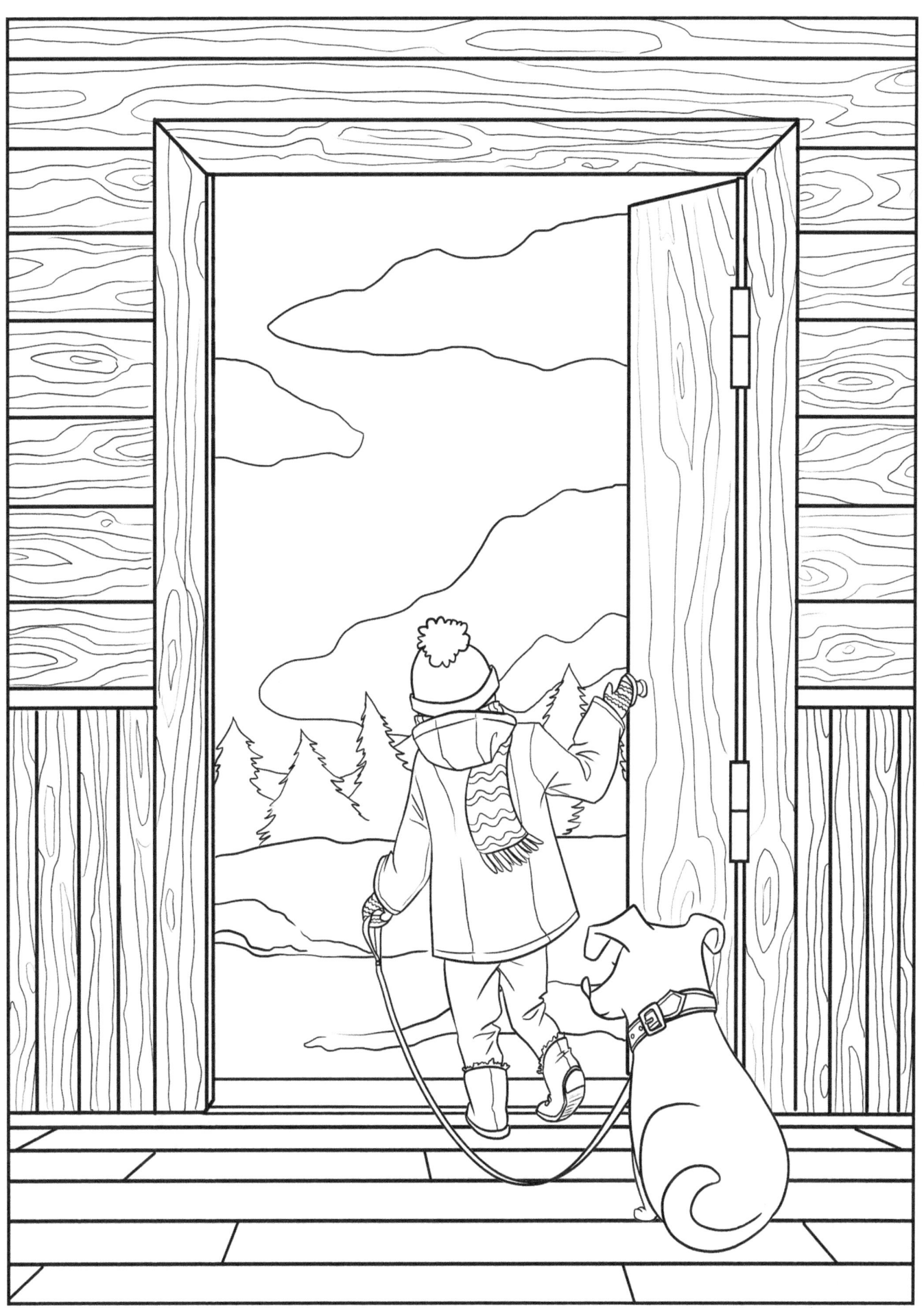

www.ingramcontent.com/pod-product-compliance
Lightning Source LLC
Chambersburg PA
CBHW081224170526
45165CB00009B/2939